ROSA GALLICA

ROSA GALLICA

Suzanne Verrier

Foreword by William Grant

FIREFLY BOOKS

A FIREFLY BOOK

Published by Firefly Books Ltd. 1999

First published by Capability's Books, Inc.

Second Printing

ISBN 0-913643-12-2

Published in Canada in 1999 by
Firefly Books Ltd.
3680 Victoria Park Avenue
Willowdale, Ontario M2H 3K1

Published in the United States in 1999 by
Firefly Books (U.S.) Inc.
PO Box 1338, Ellicott Station
Buffalo, New York 14205

Design and Production by Stanton Publication Services, Inc.
Printed in China

Front cover photograph: 'Rosa Mundi'
Back cover photographs: 'Complicata', 'The Bishop'
Picture credits: Louise Clements, page 109 ('William Grant'). All remaining photographs by Suzanne Verrier.

Heartfelt thanks to everybody that helped with this book, especially: Bill Grant, Mike Lowe, Fred Boutin, Trevor Griffiths, Eric Unmuth, Glen Jenks, Stacy Verrier, Paulette Rickard, Kristen Gilbertson, Myra Johnson, Greg Lowery, Ed Wilkinson, Dr. Wernt Grimm. My thanks also to the helpful staff at the following nurseries: Rosen von Schultheis, Ingwer J. Jensen, Rose & Rose Emporium. And to many other knowledgeable people for their very valuable assistance.

Whether by genes, with intent, or by example of joy in their gardens—my parents bestowed upon me a love of gardening which I can remember before words, and as poignantly, remains with me this day. Immeasurable pleasures and happiness their gift has brought me.

My book is dedicated with love to my parents,
Valda and Robert Verrier.

Contents

Gallic Renaissance

Several years ago Martyn Rix and I were in a procession outside the renowned rose garden at Cavriglia in Tuscany. We were part of a group that climbed a hill to a shrine where the crops were to be blessed. The group, mostly peasants, was singing a litany of saints, and Martyn and I were nudging one another every time we spotted *Rosa gallica* blooming alongside the road. How appropriate that the greatest of all European wild roses should be joining the celebration.

These roses were the typical small shrubs with light green leaves, wide light red blooms. And fragrant. I was thrilled as I had never before seen the rose in the wild.

So this was the ancestor of all my lovely Gallicas!

And now I can read about all the children in great detail. Suzy Verrier has done a scholar's research. No one before has compiled so much information about one rose. Her previous book, *Rosa Rugosa*, changed the planting habits of many rosarians around the world by showing how wonderful rugosas were for the ordinary garden. I hope all the nurseries that sell Gallicas are prepared for the rush of orders once this book is in the hands of their customers.

Only one who has written a book like this can imagine the detailed research that is necessary. The names of the roses alone required extensive searches through books and libraries around the world. So many old roses have romantic stories attached to them, and this is especially true of the Gallicas. As a lover of opera, I found many names based on the composers, the titles, and the characters. And so many plots of the grand operas employ these lovely flowers as part of their development.

Verrier has written a concise but thorough analysis of their strengths, their uses in any garden, their propagation and maintenance. Re-reading her introduction several times, I could not think of a question that she had not answered. And her rousing plea for growing these and other roses without sprays or chemical fertilizers should not fall on deaf ears.

In the years to come this book will be listed as an essential source of information about the Gallicas. No doubt there will be deletions, additions, and corrections to future editions, but there is no doubt in my mind that this is the definitive work on this lovely rose and its descendants.

BILL GRANT

Introduction

WHY GALLICAS? Fundamentally I must confess to being predisposed to all things French, whether by choice or not, for my father is a Breton, and the blood of my ancestors from this Celtic-speaking region of Brittany dictates the above. Gallica roses are French roses. Although the histories of the Gauls and the Gallicas are veiled equally behind the mists of time, no one can doubt that both flourished in France.

Where the species *Rosa gallica* originated and when it arrived in France are questions that remain unsolved. The answers will not lessen the impact of the French. They embraced and nurtured these beautiful shrubs to the extent that the Father of Modern Botany acknowledged the relationship when naming the species. In the century after Linnaeus, the lineage of *R. gallica* would truly blossom—as the garden Gallicas. Collected by royalty and created by nurserymen, these roses reached a level of popularity not to be matched until twentieth-century gardeners were conquered by the hybrid teas. The names on the following pages speak clearly of the important role that the French have played in the history of Gallica roses.

The above boast aside—a trait well documented as being a Gallic one by Caesar, these roses are a noble race, tested throughout time by garrisons of gardeners. The French Roses have resisted the ebb and flow of horticultural taste and fashion. Each day more and more gardeners discover anew the hardiness, beauty, and fragrance of these old roses. And, my intent with this book is to kindle further that already smoldering fire.

What are my qualifications for such a campaign? I am not a botanist, a geneticist, an etymologist, an archaeologist, or a historian—all possible professions of the person who may ultimately solve the mysteries of these roses. It does not call upon my ancestral bravery, however, to state very simply, "I am a time-tested gardener." Are the first-hand experiences of a gardener sufficient to evaluate the divine beauty, fragrance and hardiness of plants? I am qualified if through my descriptions and tidbits of knowledge I can ignite a passion in others similar to my own for Gallica roses. The reader must decide. Success will be mine if gardeners who share the sheer euphoric love of growing things find these roses to be exemplary shrubs. The gardener will be sublimely rewarded by the beauty of the Gallicas. *Vae victis!*—Woe to the conquered!

So proclaimed the Celtic leader Brennus after burning Rome in 390 B.C. Two thousand, two hundred, twenty years later, a crimson Gallica rose was named in his honor. This rose, which remains in cultivation, and the other Gallicas can add history, myth, and mystery as well as beauty to today's gardens.

History, Myth, and Mystery

"Lack of direct evidence, faulty reporting by the Romans, and, twenty centuries later, Romantic distortions."
—Albert Guérard, *France: A Modern History*
([Ann Arbor: The University of Michigan Press, 1959] 24).

HISTORIAN GUÉRARD'S LAMENT on the problems of French protohistory applies to the study of most things ancient. Very few facts are set in stone; most information is open to deliberation. Fluid, our understanding of history changes with new knowledge: it is affected by the perspective of the viewer; it is dependent on the words of others. Myth and romantic legend can be truthful—or at least helpful—because through such stories history becomes pertinent and understandable. Sadly, truth can also be lost in myth making.

Having read the preface, the reader will know that I am not the person who will solve the myriad of mysteries that surround Gallica Roses. Instead, what follows in this section is a composite of currently accepted facts, possible avenues of investigation, alerts to the pitfalls in early references, and helpful myths. Historians, forgive me! The romantic stories are included because these tales heighten the allure of these remarkable roses.

The ancient Gallicas are inextricably twined with the history of the genus *Rosa* itself. Where does one seek the first Gallica? Many scholars place the origin of *Rosa gallica* in the Caucasus. This mountainous region between the Black and Caspian Seas is the same geographic area where mankind perhaps first gave a name to the rose. Not coincidentally, this land is also considered a cradle of humanity.

These conclusions have partially evolved through the studies in historical linguistic change. Etymology traces language through root words, focusing on the similarity of words between cultures and the frequency in which they occur. "Rose" is recognizable in many ancient and modern Western languages, from Gaelic (*ros*) to Dutch (*roos*), from Latin (*rosa*) to Czech (*ruze*). The Celtic word *rodd* or *rhudd*, believed by some scholars to be the root of our word "rose," forms a bridge back to other earlier words. For example, the Greek *Rhodon* is visible in the name of the Aegean island famed for its Colossus and its rose production, Rhodes. Ultimately, the first word in the parent-language Indo-European for roses, *ward* or *vrod*, would have been heard in or near the Caucasus. (Readers interested in this aspect of rose history will find an excellent summary and bibliography in Gerd Krüssmann's *The Complete Book of Roses*.)

Words are helpful but what about more direct evidence—

plants. Only a definitive fossil-find would illuminate the dark corners of the centuries by providing physical proof of where *R. gallica* grew. To date, no specimen has been unearthed.

If not in fossilized form, is evidence to be found in living roses and their distribution patterns? Some botanists claim *R. gallica* is native to and still grows in southern Europe and eastward to the Caucasus. However, a debate over the exact traits of the original wild form continues, and many authorities state that the true species of *Rosa gallica* has never been found. Botanists and their work—the only possible provenance for such diametrically opposed views! In all fairness, to understand why this dispute rages is to acknowledge the potential for diversity found within this species. (By comparing the species as sold today with two of the oldest garden Gallicas, 'Tuscany' and the Apothecary Rose, gardeners will immediately appreciate the shared species traits as well as the genetic potential of *R. gallica*.)

Agreement is reached on certain points: *R. gallica* is considered to be a very old species, and its variations as well as its naturally occurring hybrids are distributed throughout Europe and in western Asia. The low-growing—almost dwarf—*R. gallica pumila* (*R. austriaca pygmaea*), which bears single red flowers, grows wild in Spain and Italy. The naturally occurring hybrids *R. x marcyana* (*R. gallica* x *R. tomentosa*, Europe, Asia Minor, Russia) are found in the south of France and have mid-sized single pink blossoms on two- to four-foot shrubs. In northern Italy, *R. x polliniana* (*R. arvensis* x *R. gallica*) is a tall shrub, bearing single, blush white to mid-pink, fragrant flowers. The distribution range of *R. arvensis* is southern Turkey to southwest and central Europe. Crosses of *R. canina* and *R. gallica* are native to woodland borders in central Europe. These produce blooms in various pink shades and foliage that shows the influence of both parents. Either di-

rectly or through its hybrid *R. damascena*, *R. gallica* is in the ancestry of *R. x alba*, found in western Asia.

Furthermore, *R. gallica* is generally accepted to be an ancestor of the Damasks, Centifolias, Mosses, and Albas. Its genes are found in countless roses, from less-known crosses of garden origin (*R. collina* and *R. x andersonii*) to those enjoying great popularity today (some of the English Roses). Unquestionably, *Rosa gallica* is in the lineage of practically all modern garden roses.

Were roses as sought after as gold, early archaeology might have yielded helpful findings in the search for *R. gallica*. Plant material was not saved or studied until modern archaeology emerged, an often cited example of which is the pivotal 1888 findings of Sir William Flinders Petrie. A photograph thrilling to rose historians appears in *The Quest for the Rose*. In it, a fresh *R. x richardii* (*R. sancta*, The Holy Rose), a cross of *R. gallica* and possibly *R. phoenicia* or *R. abyssinica*, is placed near the ancient dried roses of the Petrie expedition for comparison.

Another archaeological find in Egypt—one detailed by Mrs. J. O. Johnson in the 1947 *American Rose Annual*—is less often mentioned. Excavated in the 1940's, the tomb predated the one unearthed by Petrie. Dating from the third century B.C., it contained the diminutive mummy of a female magician, Myrithis. Masses of rose petals, blooms, buds, wreaths, and garlands were buried with her to aid her practice of white magic in the afterworld. A border of bright crimson five-petaled roses adorned her embroidered ceremonial robe. Although exact identification of the dried roses and the decorative ones is difficult, most likely *R. gallica* was the rose of Myrithis.

When turning from physical evidence to the written word, one immediately encounters greater difficulties in the search for *R. gallica*. Many red-rose references are found in early religious and medicinal texts. However, before embarking on this thorny path, the following Arabian fable on the birth of red roses should be recalled: A rebellion amongst the flowers began when the flowers tired of their queen. The drowsy Lotus had refused to revel in the moonlight, closing her petals instead. The flowers called upon Allah the Compassionate to create a new queen, and Allah produced a beautiful white rose. The nightingale, intoxicated with such beauty, flew at once to embrace the rose, but the thorns of the new queen stabbed the bird, who then bled to death, turning the petals red. The beauty of finding red roses in the texts of the ancients is irresistible; the need to read the references carefully is paramount.

Readers of Graham Stuart Thomas' books (*The Old Shrub Roses* and its newest revision, *The Graham Stuart Thomas Rose Book*), which include the work of Dr. C. C. Hurst, will be acquainted with Gravereaux's account of the sacred writings of the Median fire-worshipers. Roses were used in their religious ceremonies of the twelfth century B.C.; these roses of the Persian Magi are believed to have been some form of *R. gallica*.

Roses, red and otherwise, are mentioned by many ancient chroniclers, poets, and historians, the most exhaustive of whom was the Roman Pliny the Elder. In his *Natural History*, Pliny listed and described approximately twelve roses (Book XXI). He referred to these by location: Praeneste, Campania, Milestia, Cyrene, Carthage. Scholars continue to debate which rose of Pliny is which modern rose; scholars do not debate if *R. gallica* is among those mentioned.

Writing centuries before modern botanical nomenclature, early writers considered a rose to be simply a rose as long as it was a useful one. Roses were attached over doorways and sculpted into ceiling medallions to signify the confidentiality of *sub-rosa*

conversations. Rose petals were stuffed into silken mattresses for the ultimate experience of *dormire in rosa*, or sleeping in a bed of roses. Such a luxurious use was reportedly employed by Cleopatra in her passionate pursuit of Mark Antony. (Wouldn't she have used those petals that held an intense fragrance, those of *R. gallica*?) As chaplets and later in wreaths, roses honored the gods, the households public and private, and the tombs (and spirits) of the dead.

Pliny (Book XXI, viii, 11–12) reported that the rose wreaths fashionable after the time of Serapio Scipio were made with only genuine petals fetched from India or even beyond! The smartest prize was made from nard petals, *nardi folio*. Although "nard" might have meant a fragrant plant like spikenard, why would such a plant be introduced in the middle of a discussion of roses? *Nardus* meant "perfumed balm." Pliny continued his sentence: "if these could not be obtained, an acceptable substitution was made from multi-colored silk steeped in perfume." (My mind leaps to the variously colored Gallicas.)

The most important ancient uses for roses were medicinal. Thirty or more rose-cures appeared in *Natural History* for ailments ranging from the absurd—the bite of a sea dragon—to the commonplace, headaches. For baldness or mange, a liniment was prepared by mixing the little balls (or galls) from the wild roses with bear's grease (*silvestris pilulae cum adipe ursino alopecias emendant*, Pliny, XXI, LXXIV). Because the Greek and Roman texts contained medicinal uses, these ancient books were copied and survived the Middle Ages; for their healing properties, the roses were carried and considered valuable by invading armies. These were the uses that would later secure a place in monastic gardens for roses.

Although it has been postulated that *R. gallica* as a medicinally useful plant may have found its way into gardens, via either the Romans or the early monastic orders, during the first millennium A.D., *R. gallica* emerges more clearly from the pages of history in thirteenth century. The events that would be responsible began in the last years of the eleventh century: the Crusades. Royalty and commoners alike marched from western Europe to the Middle East. The Knights of Saint John of Jerusalem, or The Sovereign Military Order of the Hospital of St. John of Jerusalem, of Rhodes, (and later) of Malta, built their hospital during the First Crusade in Jerusalem. Whether or not the Hospitallers (or *Hospitaliers*, see index) carried medicinal roses with them to the Holy Land, they would have gained knowledge (and possibly plants) from the area's physicians. Roses of unknown type were used to celebrate victories by both Christians and Muslim Arabs. Saladin, or Salah ad-Din Yusuf, who aided the Fatimid rulers of Egypt, supposedly used an essence of roses as a purgative in places tainted by the Christians in the recaptured Jerusalem. The return of one specific crusader, Thibault IV, who was King of Navarre and Count of Champagne and Brie, brought to Provins a rose destined to be known as the Rose of Provins, the Apothecary's Rose, or the rose known today as *Rosa gallica* 'Officinalis'.

The treasure from the "land of Saracens," or Syria, which Thibault carried to Provins, a town southeast of Paris, was a semi-double bright crimson or red rose. It retained its perfume in the dried petals. The apothecaries of that town initiated an industry, making medicinal preparations and other confections from *R. gallica* 'Officinalis'; the industry flourished for over six hundred years, selling its products worldwide and bestowing them upon such notables as Joan of Arc, Louis XIV, and Napoleon. As late as 1860, 36,000 kilos of Gallica petals were sent to America.

Opoix, the same physician from Provins whose early nineteenth-century writings document the town's industry, reported how the Rose of Provins became known to the English in the late thirteenth century. About 1277 the Count of Egmont (Edmund, first Earl of Lancaster), son of the king of England, had been dispatched to France to avenge a murder. After accomplishing this mission, he returned to England with red roses, the first of which Thibault had carried from Syria. The Count of Egmont as head of the house of Lancaster adopted this same rose on his coat of arms, thus the Rose of Provins also became known as the Red Rose of Lancaster.

Although this account has been questioned (See Krüssmann's *The Complete Books of Roses*), the story does offer insight into why this red rose was sometimes known as the Red Damask Rose. The name derived from a slightly twisted legend—that this rose was brought from Damascus by a crusader.

This potential name confusion—a "Red Damask Rose" tempts modern rosarians to think incorrectly *R. damescena*—is but a glimpse of the problems lurking in the herbals of later centuries and continuing through rose books of relatively recent origin. This example of name confusion is but one in a much larger briar patch with a multitude of thorns snatching and holding snippets of history often in no logical pattern. Modern readers searching the classics, early herbals, and older modern texts will encounter a garrison of names that have been applied at various times to *R. gallica*, its forms, and its varieties: the Red Damask Rose, Red Rose of Lancaster, Velvet Rose, *R. rubra*, *R. Anglica rubra*, French Roses, *R. Provincialis rubra*, *R. rubra humilis siue pumilis*, *R. Milesia flore rubro pleno*, Rose of Provins, *R. provincialis*, *R. provincialis minor*, *R. gallica parvifolia*, Province Roses (!), (confusion with) Provence Roses, *R. Praenestina variegata plena*, *R. veriscolor*, *R. gal-*

lica officinalis, the Apothecary Rose, *R. gallica maxima*, and countless others.

Often it is difficult—if not impossible—to ascertain the identities of roses listed in the early herbals. The authors arbitrarily named their roses (perhaps a clever way of protecting questionable authenticity) and often designated them by descriptive phrases. The reader should not despair but remember Pliny the Elder had already bemoaned rose problems in the first century B.C., Book XXI,x.18-19, "tot modis adulteratur/In so many ways is spuriousness possible!" (To think that historian Guérard complained only because the ancients freely substituted the words *Gauls* and *Celts*—what a bed of roses when compared to the thicket faced by rosarians!)

One last critical point about the old herbals needs to be emphasized before continuing: the drawings should also be viewed with caution. Botanical accuracy was not always a forte—or the goal—of the scribes who copied manuscripts. The art in the early herbals was very stylized. When various copies of the herbals are compared the color of the roses is found to differ. In eight manuscripts, a rose might be white, and in three others, the same rose is red! The artists who colored the patterns may have drawn on personal experience. The rose in one copy would be red if red roses were those best known by the artist. (Nicolas Barker, *Hortus Eystettensis* [New York: Harry N. Abrams, 1994]).

What does clearly emerge from the works of apothecaries such as Besler and Parkinson is that the number of varieties of Gallicas was limited. In 1629, Parkinson listed only twelve Gallicas in his *Paridisus terrestris*. Gradually, the availability of Gallica stock and the newly increasing knowledge of the methods and mechanics of plant breeding united and gave rise to many new varieties. In the 1700's the Dutch horticulturists delved into the breeding of the Gallicas on a grand scale. The Gallicas would reach their pinnacle of popularity in the period from the early to the mid 1800's. In 1848, William Paul tempted gardeners with 471 descriptions of French Roses in his book *The Rose Garden*. (This was only a fraction of those in existence!)

The central character in the modern history of Gallicas was neither a crusader nor a druggist but instead a willful, colorful, and talented woman, Marie-Josephe Rose Tascher de la Pagerie of Martinique. In 1796, she married Napoleon. Joséphine, the name Napoleon preferred, had been known as "Rose" to intimate friends and family. Was it this name that predisposed her to a love affair with roses?

At her estate, La Malmaison, Joséphine amassed a most impressive collection with the help of her agents who had scoured Europe and beyond for all the known rose species and varieties. Neither war nor annulment of her marriage to Napoleon deterred Joséphine from her goal. At their height, the gardens at La Malmaison would boast approximately 250 varieties, of which some 167 were Gallicas. Joséphine's gardens generated intense competition among gardeners, which spurred on the nurserypeople and resulted in the creation of a multitude of new varieties. Rose hybrids number in the *thousands* by the first quarter of the nineteenth century. According to Shepherd, the catalog of the rose grower Desportes "was composed of 1,213 Gallicas."

The fabled details of Joséphine's life serve to remind us that life is change, even for the Empresses among us. It is told that Joséphine nearly always carried a rose in her hand. Her charm was undeniable but her teeth were poor, and when she smiled, she would use the rose to hide her failings. Joséphine died in 1814 from a fever brought on by overexposure in a decollete gown.

The old roses, as we would call them now, and especially the Gallicas continued to enjoy popularity for a short period after Joséphine's death. Waiting in the wings were the remontant roses. These caused another revolution: From approximately 1830, production efforts were centered on the reblooming varieties of roses. Sadly, amidst the change of fashion the number of Gallicas grown, produced, and offered sharply declined. In the third edition of William Paul's *The Rose Garden*, published in 1872, only 18 Gallicas appeared. Graham Stuart Thomas in *The Old Shrub Roses* comments that "It is only the artificially created and all too numerous productions of man that fashions change in any genus." Overexposure and the fever for things new caused the demise of the Gallicas, too.

James P. C. Russell, a compatriot and friend of Mr. Thomas, remarked in *Old Garden Roses, Part Two* (1957): "though only a small fraction of the vast race of Gallica roses is to be found in our gardens today, it represents many different types, and gives a good idea of the infinite variety we have lost."

A great portion of this stout breed of Gallica roses have vanished, but that ancient genetic fabric from the Caucasus lives on. Although very few Gallicas have been created since the early 1800's, sage hybridizers do return to the generative gene pool of the Gallicas. Professor Hansen, breeding roses in North Dakota, imported the Gallica 'Alika' from Russia in 1906 to use in his breeding program. The glorious Gallica hybrid 'Schlarlachglut' was created in 1952 in Germany by Kordes. In *A Celebration of Old Roses* Trevor Griffiths illustrated and described a beautiful cross of *R. gallica* and *R. rugosa*. Currently David Austin in England is creating a new breed of roses, a number of intensely fragrant, dark velvety red roses. 'The Prince' (1990) is but one of his roses that clearly resembles its Gallica ancestor 'Tuscany'.

And many old Gallicas are in cultivation today because of their great garden merit and, sometimes, sheer tenacity. Very certainly, they are not forgotten. "Fashion may have changed but beauty, never."

Growing the Gallicas

AMONG MY EARLIEST RECOLLECTIONS are memories of days upon days spent among the flowers in my mother's gardens. There I held one-way conversations not with imaginary friends but instead with flowers. Yes, I was always sure my silent friends understood every word I spoke to them. In that early uncluttered or unfettered state of mind, did I understand more clearly that the plants, like myself, were living things. Taking root in a childhood filled with plants as close compatriots, my gardening practices and theories have grown and ripened into practical, organic principles. From what I first knew as a child, I now further know that many living creatures—toads, birds, earthworms, micro-organisms in the soil—impact the health and success of plants, and thereby ensure our pleasure from gardens. There is no need to oppose the natural world. Long ago I dubbed myself "a gardener of least resistance." (As I grow older, this phrase accumulates more and more meanings.)

Before my mother's garden, before any garden, plants survived very nicely without human help. But, at some point, men and women became gardeners and began to tinker with Mother Nature's simple designs. Many beautiful and diverse flower forms have been created by the noble pursuit of plant breeding; however, the motives and the designs behind some plant creations have not always been pure. As mankind developed chemi-cal fertilizers, pesticides, and herbicides to create an artificial state of plant health, the quest for new and unique hybrids too often proceeded without concern for those traits that provide plants with naturally strong and healthy constitutions. Consequently, we now have far too many fluffs among the flowers, particularly among the roses.

Happily, the Gallicas, most having preceded the chemical age, are not among the ranks of weak synthetic garden plants. In contrast, the stalwart Gallicas are genuinely healthy, disease-free, pest-resistant, hardy, and accommodating plants, well suited for organic gardening methods. The fact that these roses have survived through the centuries documents these accolades.

A general green-thumb rule explains their success: the simpler a plant's genealogy, the more diverse conditions it will tolerate. Species or wild roses survive almost anywhere their seeds may fall, and the garden Gallicas, not far removed from the species, possess much of the same tenacity. I've seen many old French Roses clinging on in the most inhospitable situations. Given that the gardener does not always have a perfect site for roses, the path of least resistance leads directly to the Gallicas. They are appropriate choices for a wide range of garden conditions.

Gallica roses don't demand excellent soil, are quite content in a variety of soil types, and will even tolerate drought conditions. Typical of all roses—with a few rare exceptions, Gallicas reject wet sites. However, good soil fertility and adequate water are necessary for high performance: Ideal sites produce the best plants.

Gallicas will also grow and bloom in partial to fairly shady spots. In shaded sites there is less bloom, and the darker colors of the blossoms are less intense. Unfortunately, the dark reds lose their blackish blush. But some of the paler, more delicately colored varieties, such as 'Duchesse d'Angoulême' [#1] and 'Empress Joséphine', are actually enhanced in lower light conditions: their colors become more distinct, and their blossoms last longer in the filtered sunlight and the cooler temperatures of dappled shade. And certain varieties—'Gloire de France' comes to mind—seem impervious to less sunny sites.

Hardiness or cold tolerance is a consideration for many gardeners. The hardiness range of Gallicas extends from throughout USDA Zone 4 to throughout Zone 7, and into much of Zone 8. Although some of the more complex hybrids, such as 'Constance Spry', bloom best in the warmer areas of this range (ideally, Zones 6 and 7), and the long-caned varieties, such as 'Complicata' and 'Charles de Mills', may experience cane damage in regions with severe winters, most Gallicas can be successfully grown in Zone 4. The reports that I have received from fellow gardeners in zones warmer than those mentioned above indicate that the Gallicas do not thrive in hot humid areas.

Overall, the degree of success and the quality of performance that can be expected from a particular variety of French Rose will be in direct relation to the number of requirements that are met. Light, water, and soil fertility must be provided to some extent—the better these essentials are satisfied, the more the gardener can expect in terms of quantity of bloom and ideal growth.

CULTIVATION

Roses may be purchased either bare root or potted, own-root or grafted. Check bare-root roses and remove any broken or damaged roots. Before planting bare-root roses, soak the roots overnight in a pail of water to which I recommend adding a dose of vitamin-hormone or liquid seaweed. (These natural compounds, which do not violate organic gardening principles, are sold under various brand names.) Potted roses are rarely potted deeply enough, and the graft union is usually visible. Look for a knobby growth at the junction between the roots and the branches or canes.

Despite the controversy over own-root versus grafted (and outmoded planting concepts engineered to make roses annuals), the planting method is basically the same: all roses are best planted deeply. I advocate planting the graft union or branching union at least three inches below the surface of the soil. This practice applies to all regions, cold or hot. Deep planting offers protection from freezing, sun scald, mice, moles, voles, and a host of other stresses. An added advantage follows: deeply planted grafted roses will develop their own root system from above the graft in a relatively short period of time, thus assuring that both the plant and its roots are hardy. Northern gardeners should be aware that certain roses—particularly those grown in and for the southern states—may be grafted on tender root stock.

The planting hole should not only be deep enough but also generous enough to provide a good home. Mix a handful of bone meal or rock phosphate with the soil in the bottom of the hole to promote strong root growth. Unless your soil is nothing short of ideal, I recommend mixing the original soil with compost or well-composted manure. Add this mixture gradually, tamping down each addition. This method results in a firmly planted rose, one less likely to be buffeted by wind or dislodged in any way. (So anchored, the rose can develop its tender new white roots without damage.) Do not fill the hole completely before first filling the concavity with water to thoroughly soak the surrounding soil and to eliminate air pockets. Finish filling the hole, then mound a moat- or damlike soil ring around the hole's circumference to hold future moisture. Water, again.

Adequate water is essential throughout the first growing season while the root system is being established; thereafter, except in prolonged dry periods, the Gallicas should be able to fend for themselves. In my opinion, watering from above or at ground level makes little difference. (Some say sprinkling from above is detrimental to roses. But, how else does rain fall?)

Moisture retention is one of the many virtues of mulching. Other benefits are reduced water usage, weed control, increased soil fertility, and protection from seasonal temperature fluctuations. Mulch your plants. The most successful method of mulching that I have found begins with an application of a heavy layer (15–20 sheets) of wet newspaper (wet because if dry it will scatter to the winds and drive one to distraction) over the surface of the bed or around the rose but not closer than two inches from the canes. Cover the admittedly unsightly newspaper with a two- to three-inch layer of compost or composted manure. If you lack compost or aged manure, use a layer of leaves or straw. Do not use either bark or peat moss. Bark robs the soil of nitrogen as it decomposes, and some bark sold for mulch actually contains growth inhibitors. Peat moss is not recommended because it can draw moisture away from the plant. If too heavily applied on the surface, peat moss dries to an almost rock-hard layer that prohibits water penetration.

Reapplying mulch is best done in late autumn over any leaves that may have fallen. This additional winter protection allows any newly fallen leaves to decompose during the winter months and makes the area tidy and presentable for spring. If your garden experiences harsh winters or freeze-and-thaw temperature fluctuations, protect the roses from these conditions by placing a couple of spadefuls of well-aged manure around each plant base in the late fall. This protective mound augments soil fertility and deters any mice and moles that might visit the mulched beds. The rewards of mulching are extensive.

These practices—planting with compost or well-aged manure and re-mulching each year—should provide adequate soil fertility. Assuming sufficient fertility, average drainage, and neutral to slightly acid pH, all soils will produce Gallicas with healthy foliage and glorious bloom. Clay soils are not excluded. However, mulching dramatically improves clay. Instead of drying to a rock-hard medium by midsummer, mulched clay soil remains moist and friable. In addition, mulch encourages earthworms—creatures treasured for their castings—to increase in population: their underground activities further break down heavy clay soil and add to soil fertility. Should you feel compelled to coddle your roses, use a natural fertilizer. I like to give my Gallicas additional feedings of liquid fish emulsion and seaweed concentrate in solution, early in the season and following bloom. Generously water with this mixture around the base of each rose. Your reward will be truly superior shrubs.

As for pruning, any dead wood should be removed in the

spring. To avoid the mistake of pruning out live wood do not prune until the new growth has appeared. If you wish to prune for shape, removing overly long canes or suckers, wait until after the flowering of the Gallicas in order to enjoy the full benefit of their bloom.

The French Roses are prone to suckering. This tendency can be a disadvantage where space is limited or when the suckers crowd another plant. To remove suckers clip beneath the soil level as close to the original plant as possible.

If you wish to multiply your roses—and who does not view free roses as an advantage, the suckers will root fairly easily if treated as cuttings. (In the garden, Gallica suckers have few or no roots, and therefore cannot be simply cut and transplanted.) To root the cuttings successfully follow this procedure: In midsummer, the most opportune time, cut four to six inches from the slightly woody tips of the canes. Keep these cuttings moist and cool, remove excess foliage, and then dip them into a rooting powder or solution. Find a shady area of the garden that has light soil. For each cutting poke a hole one and one-half inches to two inches deep with your finger, a pencil, etc. *Use anything but a cutting*! Carefully insert the cutting into the hole and pack the soil to hold it firmly in place. Keep the slips moist and in humid conditions. I use plastic quart bottles with the caps still on and the bottoms cut off to create mini-greenhouses. If the cuttings haven't turned brown within two weeks, you have a good chance of success. When the slips produce new growth the bottles can be removed, but be sure to keep the young roses regularly watered.

The Gallicas are among the most disease-free groups of all roses, they are rarely bothered by the more common scourges that can decimate other roses. In times of stressful weather I have seen a touch of blackspot or of mildew here and there but never enough to cause many of the leaves to drop or to discolor and never enough to damage the overall appearance of the shrub.

Gallicas also appear to be less attractive to bothersome insects. Japanese beetles are a great source of frustration to many rose growers; however, because Gallica roses bloom in early summer, their blossoms have come and gone before the beetles arrive. Aphids, sawflies, and other uninvited and unappreciated insects will occasionally visit the Gallicas. These pests rarely cause any enduring harm. Should your garden experience an aphid or a sawfly infestation, try organic solutions. Pick and squash. Or spray the roses—particularly the undersides of their leaves—with a strong jet of water. Or take the path of least resistance: the birds and the ladybugs will often do the job while the gardener is still contemplating the problem!

Having grown 600–700 rose varieties, I would rate the Gallicas as one of the easiest, most carefree groups of all roses to cultivate. Gardening entirely without chemical sprays in a cold climate (Zone 5a with an occasional severe winter bringing periods of Zone 4 temperatures, minus 30 degrees Fahrenheit), I have never lost a Gallica to winter kill or disease. In truth, I've never lost a Gallica, period. Even if you are a gardener prone to losing plants, it is unlikely any Gallica will be on your list of losses. The Gallicas are truly low-maintenance roses but roses with a high rate of return. Can you resist them?

Garden Applications

I CAN'T IMAGINE CREATING A GARDEN without roses, but gardens without roses do exist. When I meet a gardener of a rose-less realm, and if I'm audacious enough to inquire why roses are absent, I'm most often informed that roses are too disease prone, too finicky, too tender, simply, too much trouble. What sad misconceptions surround the genus *Rosa*! If only more gardeners were acquainted with the disease-free, hardy, and unquestionably low-maintenance Gallicas, these worthy shrubs would be incorporated into every type of garden scheme, from formal historical gardens to natural plantings.

Gallicas are a godsend for the earth-sensitive gardener. They are also the perfect plants for busy or pragmatic gardeners. When growing Gallicas, there is no need for either chemical sprays or high-dose fertilizers. The diseases and the pests that plague so many modern roses pose no threat to the Gallicas. And, time in the garden throughout the year is saved because the gardener does not have to pamper these once-blooming old roses to insure attractive foliage and quality bloom. Compost and aged manure are more than adequate to produce healthy French Roses. Gallicas demand so little yet profusely provide both beauty and fragrance.

Earlier I've pronounced my adherence to ecologically minded gardening, and I will assume that if the reader has come this far with me I may begin with the garden uses that appeal to those who are green of thumb and of heart. Gardening ecologically goes beyond not using caustic substances. Our gardens and our yards should be hospitable to the earth's other denizens because everything in nature is so interconnected. Gallicas can help diversify habitat for birds and other small beings: In naturalized areas Gallicas will form protective thickets. Plant them in sun-drenched areas to provide shady havens. Adding these roses to your garden improves habitat quality both above and below the ground. Throughout the season fallen foliage collects among the densely growing canes and builds a protective layer of mulch that is beneficial to earthworms and microorganisms. In borders and gardens the long-lived and hardy Gallicas create undisturbed, life-friendly areas.

Gallicas are useful in such naturalistic plantings because their twiggy, thicketlike growth is particularly appropriate. "Fine carelessness" is how Vita Sackville-West praised the tendency of old roses to travel underground as suckers and come up feet from the parent plant. A variety such as 'Alain Blanchard' possesses a simple charm similar to that of a species rose, blends well into a wild garden, and matures into an attractive specimen even in less than ideal sites. Beyond helping to supply protective cover, a number of Gallicas set decorative hips; these hips are appreciated by the birds and other small animals. Plant either 'Complicata' or, as a lower growing option, *Rosa gallica*; both yield a supply of hips.

As densely growing, undemanding shrubs, Gallicas provide attractive year-round ground cover even in areas where other shrubs and plants will not flourish. This cover can also combat erosion in difficult sites such as steep banks. Four choices for these purposes are the much-branched 'Officinalis', its striped sport 'Rosa Mundi', the bold and beautiful 'Tuscany', and the profusely blooming 'Sissinghurst Castle'.

Moving from areas where wilderness is allowed to those where design is sought for appearance and aesthetic reward, what are the options for using French Roses in gardens. Countless. The Gallicas' great charm, beauty, and heavenly fragrance should tempt even the most mono-thematic or curmudgeonly gardeners. Even the most intensely colored varieties are never gaudy and always exhibit a good balance of color between blossom and foliage, an asset to any garden. The strong hues of the blossoms—pinks, rich crimsons, and purples—can be worked to complement and augment a variety of color schemes. (Although I must admit when 'Cardinal de Richelieu' displays its magnificent purple blooms little else will be seen in the garden: All eyes will gravitate to this rose's exquisite blossoms. The engaging pink of 'Nestor' and the bold crimson of 'Quatre Saisons d'Italie' are equally captivating.) Even when not in bloom, Gallicas—by merit of handsome foliage and attractive growth habit—add a positive punctuation in the garden. Their new,

well-colored growth tips add further depth and color contrast as they appear throughout the season.

Because the French Roses are relatively compact in growth, rarely exceeding three and a half feet, they are ideal for modern small gardens and are easily placed in a perennial, a shrub, or a mixed border. Most varieties are particularly well shaped and well clothed with foliage to the ground, no knobby-knee canes requiring disguise; the Gallicas are appropriate at the front as well as in the interior of beds and borders. These colorful fragrant roses are also fundamental to the informal English cottage gardening style.

The choice of association plantings is almost endless: Siberian irises, delphiniums, daylilies, salvias. A marvelous combination in which to blend the purple-flowering Gallicas is with blue veronicas and campanulas. You will not be disappointed. Let 'Belle de Crécy' tumble with the hardy geranium 'Johnson's Blue'. Plants with gray or silver foliage are outstanding companions: *Lavandula angustifolia* ('Munstead', ideal for colder regions), artemisias such as 'Powis Castle' or *A. absinthium* 'Lambrook Silver', *Stachys byzantina* or lamb's-ears, and the gray-leafed lavender-cotton *Santolina chamaecyparissus*. For those Gallicas with tall lax growth, place them near sturdy plants or behind low shrubs to support the flower-laden stems. During the weeks of bloom, Gallicas will reward with nothing less than "a floral sight of very high order," words of praise from the plantsman so knowledgeable in both perennials and roses, Graham Stuart Thomas. Throughout the balance of the season, their healthy leaves will serve as a marvelous foliage background for all your other plants.

Although the Gallicas are generally short shrubs, the few taller Gallicas make admirable climbers. By virtue of their hardiness

'Complicata' and 'Andersonii' are useful in cold climates; there, too, 'Charles de Mills', 'Chianti', and 'Scharlachglut' are suited for use as ramblers. Gallicas can also be utilized as climbers even in difficult sites and in areas with less than ideal light. 'Complicata' is an excellent choice for a tall rose to clamber up into a small tree. The lax long-caned habit of 'The Bishop' creates a dazzling show when cascading in full bloom over a wall.

Do not deny the Gallicas a place in your gardens because their bloom period covers only a few weeks. If season-long color is a priority in your garden, I've found a solution: the Gallicas are content to be the framework for flowering vines. Particularly recommended are sweet peas and the smaller-flowered, more softly hued morning glories or clematis. Clematis easily climbs the slight canes of these roses and then, above the abundant rose foliage, will give the bushes another burst of bloom. For example, the velvety bold scarlet-crimson flowers of 'Scharlachglut' can be joined or replaced by the purple blooms of *Clematis* x *jackmanii*. To enjoy clematis and rose blossoms at the same time, combine 'Complicata' with the popular clematis 'Nellie Moser'. The Gallicas, having strong constitutions and adaptability to various light conditions, appear never to wince at being bedecked with a vine for a portion of the summer.

Another application for the Gallicas would be low hedging, perhaps interspersed, here and there, with repeat-blooming roses or shrubs that have lengthier bloom periods. 'Camaieux', 'Cramoisi Picoté', and 'Rosa Mundi' are excellent low hedgers. Interplant with English Roses and any of the shorter, repeat-flowering rugosas. English Roses bear old-fashioned, fragrant blossoms at different points in the summer, filling the hedge with additional bloom. Try the pale pink 'Wife of Bath' or the white 'Fair Bianca'. 'The Prince', deep crimson, is another choice vari-

ety. Gardeners in the colder zones might use the rugosas 'Rotes Meer' (also known as 'Purple Pavement'), 'Fru Dagmar Hastrup', its deep dark glossy green leaves to blend with matte green Gallica foliage, and the oft-repeating 'Henry Hudson'. Purists, who appreciate the glorious bloom of Gallicas, should consider a hedge of only 'Rosa Mundi', like the famous and often photographed plantings at Kiftsgate and Hidcote Manor.

Other shrubs might be combined with the Gallicas in informal hedges. Try the attractive, long-blooming gray-leaved *Potentilla fruticosa* 'Katherine Dykes'. Its pale yellow flowers are freely produced throughout the summer. Hardy in Zone 2 to Zone 7, potentillas do not need extremely fertile soil and require little care beyond renewal pruning. Another hardy shrub to try is *Spiraea* x *bumalda* 'Anthony Waterer'. Its new growth tips —brownish red changing to bluish green—combine well with the purplish tones found in many Gallica blossoms.

The Gallicas are also effective in softening harsh foundation plantings. Having more natural shapes and good color, they act as a weaver among the more rigid forms of shrubs that supply only monotonous greens to foundation plantings. 'La Belle Sultane' with its long canes and attractive foliage would add movement and color contrast. Or enjoy the color combination of the blossoms and gray-green foliage of the lower-growing 'Gloire de France'. For those seeking a bold show-stopper, the scarlet-crimson 'Scharlachglut' must be tried. Be gone monotonous greens! Combine with the usual rhododendrons, yews, or mugo pines to have a glorious color display in June and a more interesting planting throughout the year.

As the oldest roses to be cultivated in Western gardens, Gallicas by virtue of their antiquity are prime candidates for historical gardens. Furthermore, their long association with the herbalists and the apothecaries earns for the Gallicas a place of prominence in any herb garden. A plan by Elizabeth Lawrence, which appears in *Herb Garden Design* (Swanson and Rady [Hanover, N.H.: University Press of New England, 1984]), for a North Carolina knot garden was inspired by a pattern at one of the oldest medical gardens in Europe, the Botanic Garden at Padua (founded in 1545). In it, four 'Officinalis' bushes, underplanted with *Vinca minor*, mark the corners of a square that encloses a formal design of concentric circles. Gray santolina, chive, rosemary, germander, catnip and lemon balm appear in the circular areas nearest the apothecary's roses. Another idea combines chives and garlic with *Rosa gallica* in a triangular design suitable for an herb potager. This "Foul and Fragrant" planting is interestingly finished by a third point containing asparagus, its delicate foliage in delightful contrast with that of the rose. And, anyone who has interest in potpourri must have Gallicas: the petals increase in fragrance when dried.

But paramount to every other excuse I can conjure forth, the finest reason for growing the Gallicas is the sublime reward of gardening with these wonderful old roses. Bend down and bury your nose in the delicious fragrances (aromatherapy!) of the silken petals. Put a bouquet of Gallicas on the table and get to know them intimately. Though these roses may bloom only once in a season, their images remain clear in the mind throughout the gardening year.

The Descriptions

THE SPECIES *Rosa gallica* is the aboriginal source of the garden group, Gallica roses. By having a species rose as an immediate ancestor as opposed to, for instance, the more complicated ancestry of the Bourbons or the Centifolias, the Gallicas display very distinctive features. This provides the gardener with a certain ease of group identification when an unknown rose is encountered.

Identifying any rose by its blossom alone is a dangerous pursuit. More reliable hints are often provided by foliage, growth habit, and other non-blossom characteristics. Gallica roses are recognizable in any season by their multi-caned twiggy growth —in thicketlike colonies if the roses have been allowed complete freedom from pruning shears. The shrubs are naturally compact, usually no more than three feet to three and one-half feet in height and width. The canes are mostly upright and well invested with fine reddish brown prickles rather than true thorns. (Prickles grow from the bark and are easily rubbed off; thorns spring from the wood.) If Gallicas are given adequate space and light, the shrubs are well clothed in foliage from the ground to the tips of their canes. The foliage is quite distinctive: matte—avoiding the adjective dull, which it is not—rather than glossy, and colored in predominant tones of dark olive green with paler tones on the undersides of the leaves. The picture-of-health leaves are deeply veined and have serrated margins.

Gallicas are once-blooming but with a profusion of blossom rarely equaled by repeat-blooming roses. The buds are fat and frequently blunt. Buds and blossoms are borne at the ends of sturdy canes and are generally held upright above the foliage. Blossom forms range from five-petaled singles to very double quartered blossoms with many tightly packed petals. The doubles are often flattened, although some are ball shaped or globular, and a few are cupped. Other descriptive terms applied to the variously shaped blossoms are ragged, pompom, expanded, and quilled. With a few exceptions, most Gallica flowers are mid-sized and highly fragrant. A crop of hips may follow the flowers. *R. gallica* itself gives a nice display of hips; however, like those of other Gallicas, the hips wither and lose color rather quickly.

Blossom color varies greatly: crimson, purple, mauve, magenta, and intense pink with a few magnificent pale pinks among the ranks. (Somewhere in history the Gallicas were dubbed "the Mad Gallicas," clearly an allusion to the range of unique and wonderful colors found in the blossoms.) Beyond the intense hues of the single-color blooms, some blossoms are striped, others are

SINGLE

SEMI-DOUBLE

GLOBULAR

RAGGED

CUPPED

POMPON

EXPANDED

QUILLED

QUARTERED

19

spotted; some pale near the bloom center, others fade at the circumference.

And, the Gallicas are chameleons, mad description-defying chameleons. Their colors fade and change from hour to hour, from morning to evening, and from day to day. Frequently the full palette of Gallica colors can be found in a single blossom, its tones subtly changing as the bloom ages. The colors of 'Jenny Duval' provide an excellent example. Most commonly, this rose is described as "rose with violet overtones." That is correct—for one precise moment: the initial rose-pink blooms quickly become mauve and lilac, and then gray tones appear. The age of a Gallica blossom is only one contributing factor to this color parade; climate and soil also affect color display, fertile soil and cool climate producing more intense color. Strong sunlight pales the lighter colors but puts a blackish blush on the dark crimsons and purples. A particularly moist climate or an extended rainy spell seemingly washes color from the blooms. And finally, as with all flowers, the quality of light affects color perception. Variety identification by bloom color is difficult.

So after all, the color descriptions—historical as well as those following in this book—for Gallicas can never be exact but only subjective approximations of reality. To understand historical color terms one must use hindsight: During the peak of Gallica popularity, for example, blazing scarlets and true red tones did not yet exist in European roses; therefore a rose described by plantsmen of that age as *red* would not be *red* to our eyes. Today we would probably identify the color as a shade or tone of crimson. Questions must be asked. What exact color did past rosarians mean? Were the descriptions written when the bloom had just opened or as it was fading? Were observations based on a fresh rose or an herbarium specimen? It may never be known if a rose described as "rose with violet overtones" in one historical text is the same as one listed as "rose-pink fading to mauve and lilac" in a second text.

Color is but one complication; Gallica names are another. Consider that there were more than 2,000 Gallicas in their early nineteenth-century heyday and many, many more names than roses. Some varieties were given ten or more names. Worthy roses were rechristened to suit current fashion and insure popularity. A rose, originating in Holland under one name, may have been transported to a French nursery and given a new name; the same rose, acquired by yet another grower under yet another name, may have then been renamed to honor a historical person (or two!). Nurserymen are not the only ones to blame for this confusion—even the Empress Joséphine entitled (or renamed!) a bevy of Gallicas: 'L'Empereur', 'Belle Aurore', 'Majestueuse' and 'Euphrosyne'. As roses crossed national borders their names were often translated, sometimes misspelled, and perhaps shortened if not changed completely.

On the other hand, the same name was occasionally given to many different roses. In 1846, William Prince's catalog numbered seven 'Belle Herminie's, which varied in description from "purple spotted, semi-double" to "Large, crimson mottled white, very pretty." Prince and other nurserymen of the era perhaps would have found such numbering plants to be quaint but not disturbing. The practice, which could be dubbed *numerclature*, predated the stabilizing Linnaean system of plant designation. Before Linnaeus "many of the plants were known by numbers." (L.H. Bailey, *How Plants Get Their Names* [New York: Macmillan Co., 1933], 25).

From a modern vantage point, focused by strict botanical nomenclature rules and official registration procedures, this all seems quite strange and yet it must be remembered that in past ages people also had multiple names, reflecting their birthplace, occupation, appearance, and/or current residence. One man might have been known as both John Carpenter and John of Bath. Another example, given by L. H. Bailey to explain the multiple names for the Father of Modern Botany, is "Carl von Linné signed himself as Carolus Linnaeus Smolander, his province or 'nation' being Smoland . . . also as Carl Linnaeus, Carl Linné, and Carl v. Linné." (ibid., 18). And lest we forget, the tradition of renaming roses continues today. When lost roses are rediscovered and cannot be identified by variety name, study names are applied: "Crimson Gallica," "Red Run Around," or "Canary Island." Misidentifications are made, then corrected. Botanists are always at work.

"To describe a selection of these roses is no easy task, as the plants differ so little in their habits; and their flowers, though very dissimilar in appearance, offer nevertheless but few prominent descriptive characteristics." When Prince wrote these words in the first half of the nineteenth century, he summarized the problems that remain today. I offer the following descriptive list of Gallicas currently in cultivation and the annotated index of lost Gallicas with a certain trepidation. There loom large areas of gray, a multitude of unanswered questions, and many opportunities for error when offering a descriptive list of Gallicas. I can with comfortable certainty put forth that the mystery of the clan of Gallicas will never be entirely—or even nearly—solved. (And, I would greatly appreciate corrections and comments from readers for whom I have added my address to the last page of this book.)

The following descriptions of the Gallicas that are currently in cultivation focus on the unique features of each rose. Unless mentioned otherwise, all shared traits may be assumed. For example,

the size of Gallica shrubs is quite consistent, three to three and one-half feet in height and width. Similarly, USDA Zone 4 hardiness may be assumed. Variety names are followed by known synonyms in parenthesis. The numbers enclosed in editorial brackets, here and in the index, indicate that different Gallica roses were given identical names. Whenever possible, these are numbered by date. Details of origin (hybridizer, country of origin, date of introduction or first historical record) are given when known. A date designated as "before ___" indicates first historical reference only. For those Gallicas that are less frequently found through commercial sources, I have supplied location codes at the end of entries.

Roseraie de l'Haÿ, France	1
Trevor Griffiths, New Zealand	2
Mike Lowe, USA	3
The Rosarium Sangerhausen, Germany	4
Mottisfont Abbey Garden, England	5
Göteborg, Sweden	6
Park Wilhelmshöhe, Germany	7
(Moscow) Academy of Sciences, Russia	8
Huntington Botanical Gardens, USA	9

The annotated index is alphabetized letter by letter and includes brief descriptions for the lost Gallicas. Synonyms are cross referenced. The roses currently in cultivation and their synonyms appear in boldface type. Should the reader be unable to find a particular rose, remember to check under the initial French articles *La*, *Le*, and *Les*. For ease of use, the description for a lost Gallica is given under the first name or synonym to appear alphabetically with the exception of shared rose names. Descriptions of numbered shared-name entries are grouped together for ease of comparison.

To many, reading an index is akin to reading the telephone directory, but here the reader will find the wonderful complexity of the Gallicas along with historical tidbit. Among the thousands of names in this directory are some that echo an era of romanticism ('Ornement de la Natura', 'Rouge Admirable', 'Bouquet de Vénus'), honor loved ones ('Adèle Hue', 'Joséphine Parmentier'), or revive the names and legends of the Olympian gods and the Homeric heroes ('Nestor', 'Ulysse', 'Briseis', 'Cupid', 'Juno', 'Aurora'). Appropriate to the name changes of Gallicas, many transformation myths appear: 'Daphne', 'Beau Narcisse', 'Crown of Ariadne', and 'Adonis'. And there are roses named for generals, poets, politicians, statesmen, dramatists, musicians, authors, philosophers, kings, queens, nobility, mistresses, and characters from plays, operas, and novels. These fragments of knowledge are the small details that reinforce the charm and allure of the Gallicas.

ROSA GALLICA

The species has large, cupped, single flowers that vary in color from clear deep pink to soft pink. The color pales at the base of the bloom. A prominent boss of gold stamens. Summer-blooming. *R. gallica* (*R. rubra*) forms a low, freely suckering shrub to three feet in height and width. Leaves are rough, matte, toothed, and bluish green. Slender canes, fine prickles. Scarlet-orange hips. [See page 18 for other general traits.]

[Placed before the descriptions of the garden Gallicas, the following wild varieties, obscure hybrids, or naturally occurring crosses are rarely found in commerce.]

R. g. haplodonta, a wild variation of the species, is described by *Modern Roses 10* as having "simply serrate foliage and woolly styles."

R. g. pumila (*R. pumila, R. austriaca pygmaea, R. repens*, Dwarf Red Rose). Before 1789. 'Pumila' has single rose-red blossoms on a dwarf trailing or creeping one- to two-foot shrub. Currently grown in Germany, it is found in the wild in Italy, Spain, and elsewhere in Europe.

R. x macrantha hort. A hybrid, possibly with *R. gallica*, found in France in 1823. This arching, long-caned shrub bears blush white to blush pink large single flowers. Reaching eight feet, *R. macrantha* makes a lovely climbing rose. In commerce.

R. x marcyana. A number of naturally occurring hybrids found in the south of France. Mid-size, single, pink blossoms on a two- to four-foot shrub.

R. x polliniana. In cultivation by 1820, this cross of *R. arvensis* and *R. gallica* bears single fragrant blush white to mid-pink flowers. A tall shrub to eight feet. Northern Italy.

R. x richardii (*R. sancta*, The Holy Rose, St. John's Rose). The parentage of this ancient hybrid rose is possibly a cross of *R. gallica* and *R. phoenicia* or *R. abyssinica*. Wild in the East Caucasus. Large, fragrant blush pink blossoms, paling to white. Shrub to four feet. Tender. *R. x richardii* is in commerce.

ABAILARD

Abailard

('Abalard', 'Abaillard')
Sommerson, France, 1845

Crimson buds open to double, medium-size blossoms. The rounded blossoms are bright pink, heavily marbled with vivid deep pink. Reflexed petals radiate from a greenish eye at the center of the bloom. Both buds and blossoms provide a pleasing color contrast against the attractive foliage of this plant. 'Abailard' is a handsome rose. (1,2,3)

Adèle

Descemet, France, before 1814

In cultivation at Sangerhausen and Göteborg, this is probably the same rose as 'Adèle Descemet', most likely once referred to as "Adèle by Descemet." An 'Adèle' was among the roses in Joséphine's collection at Malmaison.

Adèle Courtoise

A Gallica of unknown origin. Small, very double, rose-crimson blossoms. (4)

Adèle Heu

('Duc d'Orléans', 'Henry IV')
Vibert, France, 1816

Loosely doubled, fragrant, medium to large flowers with a center of gold stamens. The color is a bright purplish rose with lighter freckles. Growth is upright.

Named after Vibert's wife who died before seeing the introduction of her namesake rose. (2,4)

Adèle Prévost

France, prior to 1848

Fragrant, large, full flowers of blush pink with more deeply colored centers. Reflexing outer petals surround erect cupped inner petals. Vigorous, upright growth. Possibly a Centifolia hybrid. (1)

A Fleurs de Rose Tremière de la Chine

Before 1848

Large, doubled and cupped, rose-crimson flowers. The petals are spotted and edged with a lighter blush of the same color. Branching growth. (1)

Agar [#1]
Vibert, France, 1843

The double, mid-size blossoms are colored dark deep rose and spotted with a lighter tint. With age lilac tones appear. The hemispherical full blooms of 'Agar' hold a tight center of yellow stamens. (1,3,4,5,6)

Agatha

(*Rosa gallica agatha*, *R.* x *francofurtana agatha*)
Prior to 1818

Questions of parentage and place of origin surround this hybrid Gallica that is perhaps a cross with either *Rosa pendulina* or *R. cinnamomea*. From Europe or western Asia.

The fragrant, richly rose-colored blossoms are doubled, quartered (with petals grouped in quarters), veined with a deeper rose hue, and tinged with lilac. The delicate petals are irregularly arranged. Foliage is elongated and gray-green. Growth is vigorous: arching, nearly thornless canes that can reach 6 feet. Graham Stuart Thomas has discussed the similarity of 'Agatha' to 'Empress Joséphine' and 'Pope Pius IX'. See notes on 'Empress Joséphine'.

THE AGATHE ROSES

In the rose literature of the last century, Agathes were considered a distinct group or section within the Gallicas. Writing in 1846, the nurseryman William Prince cited the characteristics of Agathes as "curled foliage, and pale colored, compact flowers, remarkable for their crowded petals." These roses, mentioned in *Les*

AGAR [#1]

Roses, were popularized in eighteenth-century France. At the time of Redouté, Agathes numbered about 38. This number may seem insignificant until viewed in terms of the entire collection at Malmaison. Again, over 160 of all the roses at Malmaison were Gallicas; of these, one-fourth were Agathes. By the beginning of our century, the number of Agathe roses, as listed in *Nomenclature des tous le Noms de Roses*, had increased to 63. Today only a few representatives remain in cultivation. (See index for additional descriptions.)

The name "Agathe," which lingers in the names of most but not all of these roses, has caused speculation. In *The Ultimate Rose Book*, Mr. Stirling Macoboy has linked the name to the heroine in the popular opera *Der Freischütz*. First performed in 1821, the opera was based on German legend. Dr. Wernt Grimm of Kassel, Germany, has cited another theory based on the visual appearance of the blooms: The flowers are often marbled or speckled like the semi-precious stone, agate.

Given the interest in antiquity during the early nineteenth century, the significance of the Greek word *agathos* (feminine, *agathe*) when applied to objects must have been known. (It signifies *more than good*.) Roses, so designated, would have been considered treasures. Enthusiasts of the age, so intent on collecting unique roses and so keen about double forms, may have thus grouped these beautiful treasures under a most suitable name.

Agathes, hybrids of *R. gallica*, probably originated before 1800.

Agathe Fatime

('Fatime', 'Agathe Fatima')
Descemet, France, before 1820

Not widely available, 'Agathe Fatime' offers clusters of well-perfumed, large, doubled, and mottled blooms. The color of the roses grown today under this name—bright crimson-pink—is deeper than that commonly associated with the Agathes, thus perhaps opening the possibility of modern misidentification. Moderately vigorous growth to 5 feet. (1)

The name of this rose illustrates the period's fascination with high drama. *Fatima* has three possible sources: the wife of Bluebeard from the French fables of Charles Perrault; a holy woman in the story of Aladdin in the *Arabian Nights*; or the daughter of Mohammed from whom came the Fatimids (Moslem dynasty, 909-1171).

Agathe Incarnata

Before 1815

Pale soft pink 'Agathe Incarnata' produces very round blossoms in clusters. The well-perfumed flowers are abundant. Each consists of tissue-paper-like recurved petals arranged in quarters around a green button eye. The somewhat Damask-like foliage is gray-green. Thorny canes and dense, arching growth. A rose of very delicate beauty, yet 'Agathe Incarnata' is as hale and hardy as any of the other Gallicas.

Agathe Royale

('Bouquet Parfait')
Godefroy, France, 1817

This older variety is possibly a cross between *R.* x *francofurtana* and *R. cinnamomea plena* (*R. majalis*). Extremely full, well-formed, rich cherry pink blossoms. Vigorously arching growth and downy foliage. (5)

Aimable Amie

Known in France since 1813

Profuse bloom of fragrant, well-formed, fully double flowers. Old-Rose pink with more deeply colored centers. The outer petals reflex. A tall plant, 'Aimable Amie' grows to 5 feet. A further attribute of this rose is its handsome dark green foliage. (1,2,4,6)

AGATHE INCARNATA

27

ALAIN BLANCHARD

(blossom detail and bloom display)

ALEXANDRE LAQUEMENT

28

Aimable Rouge

('La Triomphe')
Godefroy, France, 1817

Illustrated by Redouté, 'Aimable Rouge' was popular in France and Holland in the 1820's. Its rounded well-formed, fragrant, double blossoms display a tight cluster of stamens. The color is dusty purple-pink with more deeply colored shading and veining. Medium to tall growth. (2,4,5,6,7)

Alain Blanchard

Vibert, France, 1839 or before

A stunning rose and always among my favorite Gallicas! Rather large, semi-double, cupped, and sweetly fragrant flowers. At the center of each rich deep purple-crimson blossom is a large boss of gold stamens. The blossoms are spotted or dappled with lighter crimson and, if grown in a sunny location, dusted with blackish purple. This rose is also quite at home in a fairly shady location, although the color will be paler and the dappling, less obvious. Wherever it is placed in the garden, 'Alain Blanchard' never fails to garner attention. Olive green foliage and arching canes with reddish bristles.

Sometimes listed as a Centifolia—and likely a Gallica-Centifolia hybrid—this rose retains a Gallica appearance.

Alain Blanchard Panachée, a sport, is veined rather than spotted with crimson. *Panachée* translates to "striped" or "steaked."

Alaine

Robert and Moreau, France, 1849

A rose-pink Gallica. (1)

Alexandre Laquement

('Laquemont', 'Alexander Laquemont')
l'Haÿ, France, 1906

Double, somewhat globular blossoms. Well perfumed. Rich violet-crimson, dappled red. The better traits of the group have been sacrificed in this later Gallica: the foliage is less disease-free. (1,3,4,5)

Alfieri

The date and origin of 'Alfieri' are unknown, possibly developed at Roseraie de l'Haÿ. A medium-sized shrub with mid-size, double, violet-pink blossoms. Named after the famous Italian poet and dramatist, Count Vittorio Alfieri (1749-1803). (1,4)

Alice Vena

1700's to early 1800's

Large blossoms of rich mauve-purple, produced in clusters. This older Gallica hybrid is possibly a cross with either a Centifolia or a China Rose.

ANACRÉON

ANAÏS SÉGALES

Alika

(*R. gallica grandiflora*, and possibly also 'Rose Pavot' [#1])

Large, single to semi-double, bright clear crimson blossoms with a prominent boss of gold stamens. Sadly, my experience with 'Alika' is marred by having obtained less than satisfactory plants. As a result, I have not enjoyed its legendary charm and robust growth—up to 6 feet.

In 1906, this rose was brought to the United States from Russia by Professor N. E. Hansen of North Dakota. Used extensively in Hansen's breeding program for hardy roses, 'Alika' was in commerce by 1930.

Ambroise Paré

Vibert, France, 1846

Mid-size, double, rosette blossoms of dark purple-crimson. Fragrant, speckled flowers on a large shrub. (4,5)

Amélie de Mansfield

Date and origin unknown. Medium-size, full blossoms of bright and vivid rose-pink. (1)

Amitié

A pink-blend blossom. Neither widely grown nor very well documented, 'Amitié' is currently grown in South Africa and at Sangerhausen.

Anacréon

Vibert, France, before 1834

Very double, vivid violet-rose blossoms with reflexing outer petals. Although less Gallica in appearance than those of other varieties, the well-formed blooms of 'Anacréon' are lovely. Fragrant, mid-sized flowers on a large shrub. (Anacreon, a Greek lyric poet wrote of wine, love, and roses, circa 563–478 B.C. "Ah! what should we be without the rose." Ode 51.) (2,4,6)

Anaïs Ségales

Vibert, France, 1837

In the past, 'Anaïs Ségales' has been listed as a Centifolia hybrid; indeed, its beautiful blossoms are somewhat Centifolia in form and larger than those of most Gallicas. Yet, as does Graham Thomas, I place it with the Gallicas. Its flowers are composed of concentric circles of dark lilac-crimson petals, lightly streaked with rose. With age the petals fade to lilac with paler edges. Vigorous dense growth, extremely attractive dark olive green foliage, and fine reddish prickles. This rose is endowed with a very heady fragrance.

Andersonii

Hillier, England, 1912

The undocumented parentage of 'Andersonii' is assumed to be *R. canina* and *R. gallica*; it resembles a larger, more deeply colored form of *R. canina*. The single, rich pink blooms are faintly veined with deeper pink. A large shrub (7 feet by 7 feet), 'Andersonii' bears some resemblance to the Gallica 'Complicata'.

Antonia d'Ormois

('Antoine d'Ormois')
l'Haÿ, France, before 1848

'Antonia d'Ormois' is a truly beautiful rose of the most appealing pink shades. The full blush pink blossoms have deeper pink centers. With age the blossoms pale to almost white, and the petals reflex. Pleasantly perfumed. Later blooming than most French Roses, this hybrid has some Centifolia traits, but the Gallica influence dominates. Vigorous growth to 5 feet. (2,3,4,6, 8,9)

Apothecary's Rose. *See* 'Officinalis'.

Aramis

Vibert, France, 1845

Cupped, mid-sized, doubled blossoms of white-striped light rose-pink. (4)

Ariadne

Vibert, France, 1828

Medium-size, full blossoms of rich crimson-purple. Alphabetically the first among the currently cultivated Gallicas to be named after characters of classical and Homeric myth. This heroine, daughter of King Minos, was the mother of numerous children and became the leader of the Dionysian women. Did this regal wine-colored rose also produce many offspring? (1)

Arlequin

(Possibly 'Pourpre Marbré', 'Bizarre Changeant')
Paillard, France, 1837

Very doubled, mid-sized, light violet-crimson flowers, prettily marbled. (1,6)

Assemblage des Beautés

('Assemblage de Beauté', 'Rouge Éblouissante')
Fr. Annuaire, France, 1823

An abundant bloomer with mid-sized, flattened yet very doubled flowers, each with a small button eye. The extremely fragrant blooms are bright cherry crimson, flushed with deeper purple-crimson. Compact, exceedingly dense growth. Lively rich green foliage. Green canes are armed with only a few large red thorns and many fine reddish prickles, giving an almost moss-like appearance. 'Assemblage des Beautés' is an excellent, well-behaved rose. Ideal for use in a mixed border. A very pretty rose, aptly named.

ASSEMBLAGE DES BEAUTÉS

ANTONIA D'ORMOIS

Avenant

l'Haÿ, France, 1848

Large, very doubled and expanded, deep flesh pink blossoms, which pale with age. Profuse bloom and upright growth. (1)

Bacchante

Origin unknown, before 1813

Appropriately named, this wine crimson Gallica is recorded as one of the roses in Joséphine's collection at Malmaison. (1)

Baron de Gossard

Origin and date unknown. A crimson Gallica in the collection at Roseraie de l'Haÿ.

Beau Narcisse

Miellez, France, 1850

Striped purple-violet blossoms. Named after the mythical poolside youth who was transformed into a flower. (4,5)

Beauté de la Malmaison

Origin and date unknown. Mid-size, fragrant, double blossoms of deep crimson, tinged with purple.

Bellard

('Bellart')
1857

The large blossoms are well scented, doubled, and quartered, each with a button eye. Light pink with a paler border. Mid-sized shrub. (1,4,5,6)

Belle Biblis

Descemet, France, 1813

This Gallica, listed in Joséphine's collection at Malmaison, remains in cultivation at Sangerhausen and Mottisfont Abbey. Its violet-rose, mid-size blooms are lightly perfumed. Biblis is not only the name of an ancient city in Phoenicia (according to some, the oldest city in the world!) but also that of a mythic woman who was transformed into a constantly weeping fountain.

Belle de Crécy

Hardy/Roeser, France, 1829

Reputedly raised at Madame de Pompadour's chateau at Crécy and introduced in the late 1820's. Possibly a Gallica-China hybrid.

A vigorous mid-sized shrub with handsome blue-green foliage that is practically thornless, bearing only a few fine red prickles. The heavily perfumed blossoms are large and flattened; the center petals incurve around a green button eye. Crimson buds open to cerise-pink blossoms, flushed with violet. As the bloom matures, mauve and gray tones appear. James Russell in *Old Garden*

BELLE DE CRÉCY

Roses completes the description: "the pale reverse of a few incurving petals show like light reflected from the waves of a stormy sea." 'Belle de Crécy' is widely grown, and its popularity is well deserved.

Belle des Jardins

Guillot fils, France, 1872

Assumed to be a cross of 'Village Maid' with an unknown seedling, 'Belle des Jardins' displays barely double, large velvety blossoms of deep purplish crimson, occasionally streaked with white. (1,2,4,6)

Belle de Yèbles

Desprez, France, 1830

This lightly fragrant, vivid crimson Gallica remains in cultivation in Europe. (1,4)

Belle Doria

('Bella Doria')

Origin and date unknown. Cupped, doubled, mid-sized flowers of rich violet-pink, striped irregularly with dark crimson and occasionally with white. (1,6)

Belle Galathée

Descemet, France, before 1813

A flesh pink Gallica, listed as one of the roses in Joséphine's collection at Malmaison. The color of the blossoms echo the myth behind the name: a statue, so loved by Pygmalion, was turned into a woman by Aphrodite. (1)

Belle Hélène [#2]

Vibert, France, before 1813

Two separate roses appear to have been named 'Belle Hélène'. See index. Apparently, the rose currently in cultivation is the one that was grown at Malmaison. 'Belle Hélène' [#2] bears mid-sized, very doubled, cupped blossoms of rosy crimson with violet overtones.

Belle Herminie [#6]

Coquerel, France, before 1846

Well-perfumed, very doubled, mid-sized blossoms, each with a glimpse of gold stamens. The blooms are richly colored mauve-crimson at the center; however, the paler reflexed petals are shaded mauve at the circumference. Several other roses, none of which appears to be in cultivation today, have also held this name. See index. (1,3,4)

BELLE HERMINIE [#6]

BELLE ISIS

Belle Isis

Parmentier, Belgium, 1845

Unknown parentage. A Gallica with distinctly non-Gallica coloring. This rose was a parent of the well-known English Rose 'Constance Spry'.

Buds, which are brushed with deep crimson, open to doubled, quartered blossoms with reflexed outer petals and a strong fragrance. The coloring is delicate: a pale coral-pink flush over a cream-color base with a hint of soft yellow. Gray-green foliage on a compact plant. A very beautiful flower on a tidy bush!

Belle Parade

Holland, before 1813

Among the roses that were grown in Joséphine's collection at Malmaison, this violet-colored Gallica is currently at Roseraie de l'Haÿ.

Belle Pourpre

Descemet, France, before 1813

A purple-crimson Gallica. In Joséphine's collection at Malmaison. (1)

Belle Rosine

Vibert, France, before 1834

An abundant bloomer with large, double, and expanded blossoms of crimson-pink with paler edges. Moderate, erect growth. (4)

Belle sans Flatterie

Godefroy, France, 1820

Very popular in the early nineteenth century, the particularly pretty 'Belle sans Flatterie' produces very doubled and quartered, mid-sized blooms. Cool lilac-pink at the circumference and rich mid-pink at the center. Outer petals are reflexed and the centers are flattened. This rose has been known to occasionally rebloom with a few late blossoms, indicating that it is a hybrid. (1,4,6,7)

Belle Virginie

l'Haÿ, France

Date unknown. Crimson buds open to a profuse bloom of lilac-violet blossoms. Upright bushy growth. (1,5)

Béranger

Laffay, France, before 1846

Small, doubled, mottled blossoms of rosy crimson. Named after the French poet Pierre Jean de Béranger (1780-1857). (1)

Bérenice

Vibert, France, 1818

Pink and crimson blossoms with mauve shading. Large, full, globular blossoms. Vigorous spreading growth. (Famous tragedy by Racine.) (4,5)

Bijou des Amateurs

Before 1848

Mid-sized, doubled, crimson blossoms with cream-colored spots. Violet petals at the circumference. (1)

Belle sans Flatterie

BOULE DE NANTEUIL

CAMAIEUX

Blanche Fleur

Vibert, France, 1835

This Gallica-Centifolia hybrid is often listed today with the Centifolias; however, earlier references—such as *Nomenclature de tous les Noms de Roses*—include 'Blanche fleur' with the Gallicas.

A profuse early bloom of sweetly perfumed, large, double blossoms of white, tinged with flesh pink. Moderate, somewhat open growth.

Blush Gallica

Details of date and origin are uncertain. An old early flowering lilac-pink Gallica with more deeply colored centers. The blooms are doubled and loosely quartered. (1,2)

40

Bossuet

1857

Double, crimson blossoms with a darker circumference. Named after a famous seventeenth-century French bishop. (1)

Boule de Nanteuil

('Comte Boula de Nanteuil')
Roeser, France, 1834

Aptly described by William Paul as "a splendid Rose." Very large and very doubled, fragrant, flat, quartered blossoms, each with a small bunch of gold stamens. The color is deep crimson-purple with silvery overtones. Moderate branching growth. (1,2,3,4,6)

Bouquet Charmant

('Vénus Mère', 'Bouquet Superbe')
Guerrapain, Holland, before 1834

Large, double, vivid rose-pink blossoms. (1)

Bouquet de Vénus

Lerouge, France, date unknown

Large flowers of soft blush pink, doubled and quartered, each with a button eye. Well perfumed. (1,4,6)

Brennus

Laffay, France, 1830

Although classified sometimes as a Hybrid Bourbon, a Hybrid China, or a Gallica, this non-remontant rose displays many Gallica traits in its appearance. Its double crimson blooms are shaded violet. See index for 'Couleur de Brennus'.

Camaieux

Vibert, France, 1830

One of the best striped roses. The well-formed, barely doubled blossoms have neatly arranged petals, which slightly reflex. The ground color is pale blush pink, almost white, and is neatly and distinctly striped with dark rose. Aging, the colors pale to white with violet-purple, mauve, and lavender-gray. 'Camaieux' is sweetly perfumed. Its well-shaped growth is compact, usually no more than 3 feet in height.

Camaieux Reversion, a recent sport of 'Camaieux', has unstriped blossoms of dusky mauve.

Canary Island

(Study name)

A study name is a temporary one given to a rose when its true identity or original name has been lost. This rose with distinctly Gallica characteristics was rediscovered in San Antonio, Texas. The study name summarizes its known history: it was transported to the Texas coast from the Canary Islands in the 1920's.

Double, lavender-pink, fragrant blossoms on a 4- to 6-foot

CARDINAL DE RICHELIEU

shrub. The thin canes have few prickles. When grown in a cold climate, growth is considerably smaller. Quite likely a Gallica hybrid.

Capricorne

('Capricornus', 'Capricorn')
Miellez, France, 1838

Very double, convex mid-size blossoms, vivid pink in color. Described by Gore. Identification of the rose currently in cultivation is tentative. (4)

Captaine Williams

(Captain Williams)
l'Haÿ, France

Lightly fragrant, mid-size, very double, dark crimson flowers on a medium-sized bush. (1,4)

Cardinal de Richelieu

Laffay, France, 1840

Likely a Gallica hybrid with perhaps some China Rose in its background. Created by Van Sian in Holland and sent unnamed to Laffay.

'Cardinal de Richelieu' offers outstanding flower color and form. Clusters of fat, round, deep crimson buds open to vivid deep purple blooms that mature to dusky lilac. The petals pale to near white at the base, incurve at the center of the flower, and reflex at the circumference. Certainly, one of the most purple roses grown and aptly described by Graham Stuart Thomas as having "the sumptuous bloom of a dark grape." 'Cardinal de Richelieu' is an eye-catcher and a tough little rose with long-lasting blossoms. Its only drawback—and one which should not deter you—is a slight tendency to blackspot.

This rose is named after Louis XIII's minister—a prominent ecclesiastic and powerful statesman.

Carmine Brilliante

('Carmin Brillant')
l'Haÿ, France, before 1813

Double, rich carmine blossoms. A Gallica of uncertain origin that was in Joséphine's collection at Malmaison and is now in cultivation at Roseraie de l'Haÿ.

Catinat

Robert, France, before 1846

Very doubled, cupped, mid-sized blossoms. Mauve-purple blend, spotted cream. Vigorous, upright growth. (4,5)

Césare Beccaria

Robert and Moreau, France, 1870

Large full blossoms, variegated white and violet, on a medium-sized shrub. (4)

Chapelain d'Aremberg
('Chapelain d'Arenberg')

Origin and date unknown, possibly originating at l'Haÿ in France. A full, vivid rose-pink Gallica. (1)

Charles de Mills
('Charles Mills', 'Charles Wills')

'Charles de Mills' seems to have originated in Germany as 'Charles Wills'; its name changed on its arrival in France. Although sometimes said to be 'Bizarre Triomphant', the descriptions of that rose are significantly different. (See index.)

However obscure its history may be, today this is a well-known rose by virtue of its singular and handsome garden demeanor. The large blossoms have the appearance of textured velvet: very doubled, many petaled and quartered. The color is vivid purple-crimson, deepening in the center and aging to maroon, lilac, and mauve-gray. Now if you can imagine the blossoms trimmed with hedging shears—Snip, snip—you can visualize the flattened form of these circular flowers. Add a pale green eye at the center. Vigorous arching growth to 5 feet in height, yet well mannered and particularly beautiful. 'Charles de Mills' is a welcome addition in any garden.

Charles Quint
Robert and Moreau, France, 1887

Blossoms of lilac-rose and white. (1,4,5,6)

Château de Namur
Quetier, France, 1845

A hybrid Gallica with doubled blossoms, palest pink to near white, finely striped with soft rose. Intoxicating perfume. (1,2,6)

Chaucer
Austin, England, 1970

This modern English Rose—one of David Austin's earliest introductions and the parent of many of his later roses—receives Old Rose characteristics from its Gallica-hybrid parents, 'Duchesse de Montebello' x 'Constance Spry'. (See individual entries.)

Doubled, cupped, and globular flowers of flesh pink color with deeper roseate centers. A myrrh scent. Small to medium upright growth. This lovely rose is somewhat tender for cold northern gardens and often suffers in severe winters in USDA zone 5.

Chénédolé
Thierry, about 1840

This Gallica-China hybrid, often listed as a Hybrid China and likely a first-generation cross, clearly retains many Gallica traits. The particularly large, very doubled, and cupped flowers of bright glowing crimson are non-recurrent.

This rose was named for a member of the Chamber of Deputies in Calvados, Normandy.

CHARLES DE MILLS

CHIANTI

Chianti

Austin, England, 1967

Created from the Floribunda 'Dusky Maiden' and one of the finest and oldest Gallicas, 'Tuscany', this modern English Rose hybrid has blossoms that are truly Gallica in character. The large, double, very deep wine crimson blooms that age to purple-crimson are heavily perfumed. 'Chianti' makes a stunning rambler-type shrub with vigorous growth, reaching 5 feet or more. Beware, it tends to suffer a bout with blackspot immediately after bloom; however, its vigorous nature prevents any lasting damage.

Chloris

Descemet, France, 1800

Gardeners need to be aware that the rose usually sold under this name today is the pink Alba, also known as 'Rosée du Matin'. Reported in the current inventory of Roseraie de l'Haÿ, the French Rose 'Chloris' is a Gallica of unexpected color—white.

Must we restrict Gallicas to the colors pink through purplish crimson? My vote falls with Graham Thomas' comment in *The Old Shrub Roses* on curiously not finding a white variety: "This is rather surprising." The potential surely is in the Gallicas: white appears in strips, streaks, and spots. Could these now mysteriously missing roses, perhaps arising as sports or mutations in the same manner as the randomly appearing variegated Gallicas, have once been held in high esteem as oddities? Then replaced by more worthwhile later white introductions? (Indeed, a 'Chloris' was listed in Joséphine's collection.) This rose and a few other Gallicas were described in the nineteenth-century listings as "white," while roses of less than pure white were accurately noted. For example, 'Blanche fleur' with its misleading name was described as "white, tinged with flesh pink."

The name itself, providing no clue, does interestingly reflect on the name-change mess encountered when researching historic roses. Absent from most modern mythology texts, Chloris, too, has been all but lost. This was the Greek name for Flora, the goddess who spoke with rose-scented breath, whose name was corrupted as it passed into Latin. (Ovid, *Fasti*, v. 195.)

Cocarde Pâle

Pradel, France, 1820

A Gallica with light rose-pink blossoms grown at Roseraie de l'Haÿ.

Columelle

('Columella')
Robert and Moreau, France, 1860

Medium-sized, doubled, and cupped blooms of rich crimson-rose with a slight flush of violet at the edges of the petals. Branching growth. Sometimes listed as a Damask, 'Columelle' is most likely a hybrid Gallica. (1)

Complicata

Reminiscent of the species *R. gallica*, the five-petaled flowers are large and bright pink, paling toward large centers of yellow stamens. This rose is perfectly wonderful in full bloom. Gray-green foliage adorns the plant, and the upper portions of the canes are nearly thornless. Globular orange hips. Useful for growing into trees, the rambling 'Complicata' is quite tolerant of shady conditions.

The name perfectly expresses the ambiguous parentage of this rose and explains aspects of its appearance. The single blossoms are on vigorous long-caned growth to 10 feet, atypical of the Gallicas. Its origin and date are unknown; 'Complicata' is possibly a Gallica x *R. macrantha* hybrid. *R. canina* and the North American rose *R. setigera* have also been suggested.

C O M P L I C A T A

Comte Foy de Rouen [#1]
Savoureaux, France, before 1836

Very large, double, fragrant flowers of a pale rose color. (1)

Comtesse de Lacépède
Duval/Verdier, France, 1840

Various texts agree that 'Comtesse de Lacépède' is a Gallica hybrid, probably with a China Rose. William Paul, a nurseryman and rosarian, described 'Comtesse de Lacépède' as "delicately beautiful," and its blossoms as large, full, cupped, silvery white (or white with a blush). Now in cultivation at Sangerhausen, this rose is described as "dark red, medium-sized." Misidentified?

Conditorum
(*R. gallica conditorum*, 'Tidbit Rose', 'Hungarian Rose')
Dr. Dieck, Prussia, 1900

An ancient rose, reintroduced in 1900. Richly perfumed, large, semi-double flowers of deep crimson with purple overtones and glimpses of gold stamens. The blossoms bear a resemblance to both *Rosa gallica* 'Officinalis' (the 'Apothecary's Rose') and 'Tuscany'. Dark green foliage and upright growth. (2,5,6,10)

In German, *konditorei* refers to confectioners' shops where cakes are decorated with candied rose petals. Did someone latinize this word for an apt name?

Constance Spry
Austin, England, 1961

Mr. Austin's first English Rose, 'Constance Spry' resulted from a cross of the Floribunda 'Dainty Maid' with the Gallica 'Belle Isis' (See entry).

The large, cupped, globular, rich mid-pink blossoms are heavily perfumed with a myrrh fragrance. Strong, vigorous, long-caned growth to twelve feet.

This rose is a good example of the valuable assets that Gallicas bring to the breeding of interesting modern roses. However, the Gallica trait of blooming on old wood when combined with the greater tenderness of Floribundas, as in 'Constance Spry', prevent cold-climate gardeners from fully enjoying such roses. For dependable performance from year to year, 'Constance Spry' is best grown in moderate climates, USDA Zone 6 and warmer. Yet, this is such a lovely rose, and I have grown 'Constance Spry' in a cold Zone 5 garden with ample yet sporadic reward.

Cora
Sauvoureux, France, before 1885

Clusters of small, well-formed double blossoms of rich velvety violet-purple. The bases of the petals pale to white. Moderate erect growth. (Another name in mythology for Proserpine, the daughter of Ceres and wife of Pluto.) (2,4,5,6)

Cosimo Ridolfi

('Casimo Ridolphi')
Vibert, France, 1842

Handsome, mid-sized, cupped, dusky lilac-rose blossoms, mottled and veined with crimson. The very full flowers are well formed around tight centers of gold stamens. Well perfumed. Gray-green foliage on a compact, well-behaved shrub. (2,4,5,8)

Cramoisi des Alpes

('Monsieur', 'Grand Corneille')
Belgium, Prior to 1838

An abundant bloom of double, mid-size, vivid crimson-purple blossoms on rather long flower stalks. (1)

Cramoisi Éblouissant

Before 1813

A crimson Gallica currently grown at Roseraie de l'Haÿ and formerly in Joséphine's collection at Malmaison.

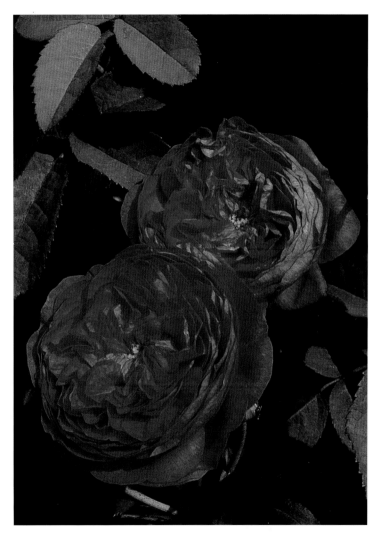

COSIMO RIDOLFI

49

CRAMOISI PICOTÉ

Cramoisi Picoté
Vibert, France, 1834

A good example of the ranunculus-flowered Gallicas. Blunt, fat, crimson buds seem to explode into small, very doubled blossoms, tightly set with neatly arranged petals. Rich lilac-rose, marbled with crimson and paling to lilac. Small, exceedingly dark green foliage on compact, almost dwarf, growth. And, a very pleasant light fragrance. 'Cramoisi Picoté' is a little charmer that well illustrates the varied allure of the Gallicas.

Cynthie [#1]
Descemet, France, before 1815

Large, doubled, nicely formed, cupped, light rose-pink blossom with a blush circumference. Profuse bloom and upright growth. (Another name for the goddess Diana and for the moon.) (4)

d'Aguesseau
Vibert, France, 1823

Particularly vivid violet-crimson blossoms, shaded with purple when grown in a sunny location. The color is very fine—one of those delightfully clear bright colors not readily found in the plant kingdom—wonderful in combination plantings or equally effective as an accent in the garden. The fragrant flowers are well formed, doubled and quartered, with reflexing outer petals. Handsome dark green foliage and vigorous erect growth to 5 feet.

D'AGUESSEAU

Daphné [#1]
Vibert, France, 1819

Doubled rosette-formed blossoms of rich lilac-pink, each with a small, barely visible, yellow eye of stamens. A tall-growing shrub. (See index for additional comment.) From myth, Daphne was changed into a laurel tree by Apollo. (2,4,5)

Désirée Parmentier

Before 1848

Possibly a Centifolia hybrid, one probably developed by Parmentier in Belgium. Large, very doubled, and well-formed blossoms of bright rich rose. Petals reflex and pale slightly at the circumference. Dense branching growth. (1,3,9)

Dometille Beccard

France, before 1857

Mid-size, double, fragrant blossoms of vivid pink, striped with white. Medium to vigorous growth. (1,4)

Doña Sol

Vibert, France, 1842

Possibly a Gallica-Centifolia hybrid. 'Doña Sol' has large, well-doubled, violet-crimson blooms, spotted with white. Vigorous growth. (1)

Double Brique

1830

Details of origin for this rose, likely from France, have been lost. Double, rose-pink blend with silvery shading at the circumference of blossoms. (1,3,4,6)

Swirling around 'Duc d'Angoulême' and 'Duchesse d'Angoulême' are a host of synonyms, many of which also apply to other roses. The definitive answers to this confusion are lost in time, but my attempt to clarify follows. (For the sake of clarification, the 'Duchesse d'Angoulême' has been removed from alphabetical order to be placed with 'Duc d'Angoulême'. Also, see index entries.)

The Duc d'Angoulême was a Bourbon prince in the Napoleonic era. Both he and his wife shared a keen interest in gardens; however, the roses named after them are distinctly different.

Duc d'Angoulême [#1]

('Duc de Bavière' [#1], 'Duke of Bavaria', 'Lady Peel', 'Reine de Prusse' [#1])

Possibly a Gallica hybrid, this rose appears to have originated in Holland in 1824 and then reintroduced by Vibert in 1835. The deep lilac-pink blossoms are double.

Désirée Parmentier

53

DUCHESSE D'ANGOULÊME [#1]

Duchesse d'Angoulême [#1]

('Reine de Prusse' [#2], 'Agathe Marie Louise',
'The Wax Rose', 'Agathe Précieuse')

A hybrid Gallica, possibly crossed with an Alba or a Centifolia. The date of introduction appears to have been 1827. Both Miellez and Vibert have been credited with this rose; Hardy has been associated with 'Reine de Prusse' [#2].

Cupped and nodding, the blooms have slightly recurved petals. The translucent quality of the petals echo its name, The Wax Rose. The color also has an ephemeral quality—a center of blush and silvery lilac-pink, paling to almost white at the border.

Duc d'Aremberg

('Prince d'Aremberg')

Clusters of large double blossoms of bright rose-pink with outer petals of lilac-pink. An upright vigorous shrub. Although now in cultivation at Roseraie de l'Haÿ and possibly developed there, the origin and date of this rose are unknown.

Duc de Bordeaux

Vibert, France, 1820
(Possibly originally from van Eeden, Holland, or earlier)

Large double blossoms of uniform lilac-rose color. (1,4)

Duc de Fitzjames

France, before 1885

Extremely doubled, cupped blossoms, beautifully formed with tightly packed petals. The bright, richly colored deep violet blossoms are borne in clusters and are heavily perfumed. Matte olive green foliage. New growth is interestingly tinged with a rust color. A picture-perfect Gallica. (3)

DUC DE GUICHE

Duc de Guiche

('Sénat Romain')
Prévost, France, before 1813

A fragrant, large, cupped, quartered, and globular flower of vivid violet-crimson veined with a deeper hue. A green button eye. As the blossom ages, the outer petals reflex and the center changes to deep violet. This particularly handsome shrub has bright green foliage and vigorous arching growth. Now in cultivation at Roseraie de l'Haÿ and Sangerhausen, 'Duc de Guiche' was grown at Malmaison.

56

Duchesse de Berry [#1]

Vibert, France, 1825

Neatly formed rosettes of wavy frilled petals. Loosely double, large flowers of lilac-rose, streaked with mauve-crimson. Well perfumed. Tall vigorous growth without prickles and few, if any, thorns. This rose is sometimes listed as 'Duchess de Berri'. (4,6)

Duchesse de Buccleugh

Robert, France, 1846

Late-blooming among the Gallicas. Large, doubled, flattened, and quartered blooms of vivid deep pink, each with a green eye. A prolific bloomer and vigorous grower, this dense shrub reaches 5 feet. Attractive gray-green foliage. (1,2,3,4,8)

Duchesse de Montebello

Laffay, France, 1829

A Gallica-China hybrid, sometimes classified as a China. Doubled and perfectly quartered, small to mid-size blossoms with a light sweet scent. The color is soft coral-rose, paling with age to flesh pink. An early bloomer with compact growth and gray-green foliage. (The Duchesse was the wife of Maréchal Lannes, a soldier who was honored by Napoléon with the title Duc de Montebello and after whom other roses were named.)

DUCHESSE DE BUCCLEUGH

Dumortier

France

The details of origin and date are unknown. Possibly developed at l'Haÿ. Mid-size, very double, flat blossoms of light crimson. The color of the reverse (or bottom side) of the petals has a silvery quality. (1)

Dupontii

France, before 1817

This late-flowering hybrid has an occasional rebloom and is most often considered to be a cross between *R. gallica* and *R. moschata*. Another opinion cites *R. arvensis* as the second possible parent.

Bracts of large three-inch, single, snow white blossoms with showy prominent centers of gold stamens. The well-scented flowers are followed by orange hips. Growth is tall, achieving 8 feet in height. Green canes and gray-green foliage.

Named for the prestigious French nurseryman.

Ekta

Hansen, USA, 1927

Created by a cross of 'Alika' [See entry.] and 'American Beauty', a Hybrid Perpetual. The resulting blossoms are single, pink, and once blooming. (4)

Élise Rovella

France

A vigorous tall-growing rose with mid-size flesh pink double blossoms. Date and details of origin are unknown, possibly developed at Roseraie de l'Haÿ where it remains in cultivation today. (1,4)

Empress Joséphine

('L'Impératrice Joséphine', 'Souvenir de l'Impératrice Joséphine', 'Francofurtana', *R.* x *francofurtana*, The Frankfort Rose, 'Rosier de Francfort', *R. turbinata*)

A world of speculation surrounds this rose. One of the few points in general accord is that 'Empress Joséphine' is a Gallica hybrid, most likely of *R. cinnamomea plena* (*R. majalis*) or of *R. pendulina*. *R. cinnamomea plena* is supported by the fact that 'Empress Joséphine' is very hardy, succeeding in USDA zone 4. *R. pendulina*, often suffering dieback in a cold zone 5, is less hardy than *R. cinnamomea plena*. Although one could attribute the hardiness to the Gallica parent, other factors also point toward *R. cinnamomea plena*. 'Empress Joséphine' is distinguished by a translucent or tissuelike quality of the petals, closer to the character of *R. cinnamomea plena* than of *R. pendulina*. The wide stipules further support the theory that *R. cinnamomea plena* is the parent in question. On the other side of the debate, the alternate name, *R. turbinata* refers to the shape of the elongated hips, which more closely resemble those of *R. pendulina*. Finally, to compound confusion, both *R. cinnamomea plena* and *R. pendulina* are practically thornless as is 'Empress Joséphine'.

Scholars also agree that 'Empress Joséphine' is a very old rose. It was most likely renamed 'Empress Joséphine' after death of the Empress because no rose name containing her own was found in the lists of her collection. Krüssmann has identified it at Malmaison, from the J. Gravereaux list, as 'Rosier de Francfort' (=*R. turbinata*). But what of its earlier history. If we accept Francofurtana as a synonym for this rose, scholarship has revealed historical mentions in the late sixteenth and early seventeenth centuries. Noted in *Quest for the Rose*, the English gardener John

EMPRESS JOSÉPHINE

Tradescant the Elder (c. 1570-1638) collected Francofurtana in 1618 when he accompanied Sir Dudley Digges to Russia. Graham Stuart Thomas, in *Old Shrub Roses*, has noted that the herbalist Clusius recorded this rose in 1583.

Aside from all the controversy, the 'Empress Joséphine' is an engaging and lovely, charmingly ragged, and loosely double rose with a light sweet perfume. The blossoms are a mix of soft pink to lilac, tinged rich rose-pink with more deeply colored centers and darker veining. The leaves are deeply veined, the canes are nearly thornless, and the growth (to 5 feet) is open yet dense.

Although other roses from her collection are more striking, on seeing the delicate beauty of this rose, I must believe a story surrounding it: this was the favorite rose of Empress Joséphine.

Enfant de France [#1]

('L'Enfant de France')
Hardy, France, 1802

The origin of this rose is uncertain. Quite possibly originating in Holland before 1802, it was grown in Joséphine's collection at Malmaison. Dark rose-pink with lilac overtones, double, mid-size blossoms. This rose differs from another 'Enfant de France' [#2] ('Roi de Rome' [#2]), a rose attributed to Prévost. (6)

Estelle

Origin and date unknown. Well-perfumed, mid-pink, very doubled roses on medium to large shrub. Grown at Malmaison during Joséphine's time. (1,4)

Esther

('Grande Esther', 'Duchess d'Oldenburg')
Vibert, France, 1846

A mid-size, loosely double blossom which when fully expanded is composed of ragged quilled petals. Barely visible center of yellow stamens. The soft rose-pink blossom is irregularly and sparsely striped with vivid purple-crimson. Good fragrance and vigorous growth. (2,4)

Eucharis

Descemet, France, 1815

A hybrid with large full blossoms of light pink, flattened, and randomly striped with a deep bright rose color. A button eye. Well perfumed. Vigorous growth. (1)

Eulalie Lebrun

('Eulalia Le Brun')
Vibert, France, 1844

The mid-sized, doubled blossoms of 'Eulalie Lebrun' are variegated or mottled white, rose-violet, and lilac. Although the foliage—a little too glossy and somewhat too smooth—hints at hybrid ancestry, the blossom appearance is Gallica-like. (1,4)

Eulalie Lebrun

61

Euphrosyne L'Élégante

('Euphrosine L'Élégante', 'L'Élégante' [#1])
Prévost, France, before 1813

Semi-double blossoms of bright crimson-pink, each with a center of deep gold stamens. The outer petals are often spotted. Named for one of the three Graces, 'Euphrosine L'Élégante' grew in Joséphine's collection at Malmaison. (1)

Eveline

Origin and date unknown. A well-formed, soft but bright rose-colored, full flower with a glimpse of gold stamens at the center. Globular buds unfold to reflexed petals. Well perfumed. (2)

Fanny Bias

('Duchesse de Reggio', 'Fanny Parissot')
Vibert, France, 1819

Today 'Fanny Bias' is often associated with 'Gloire de France'. The linkage is understandable because these two roses were similarly described in early listings. However, the nineteenth- and early-twentieth-century texts, such as *The Rose Garden*, *Prince's*

Manual of Roses, and *Nom des Roses*, presented them as distinct varieties and did not link the names as synonyms. 'Fanny Bias' and 'Gloire de France' were described as subtly differing in coloration and growth habit, the former being the paler of the two. 'Fanny Bias' was considered to be a Gallica or French Rose, not a hybrid. Because the two names are now so closely tied, it must be questioned if only one or both varieties are in cultivation. (See 'Gloire de France' entry.)

Relying on the older texts, I offer the following description for 'Fanny Bias': The blush- to flesh-colored blooms have centers of a deeper rose-pink. The large blossoms are doubled and well formed with tissuelike petals. Upright growth. (1)

Fanny Essler

France, 1820

Pretty, mid-sized, rich pink, dappled, doubled blossoms on a medium-growth shrub. (1,3,4)

Fanny Pavetot

France, 1820

Vivid pink, double, mid-size blossoms with a good scent. (4)

Ferdinand de Buck

('Feu de Buck')

Details of date and origin unknown. Mid-sized, doubled blossoms of bright vivid pink. In cultivation today and possibly developed at Roseraie de l'Haÿ.

Fleurs de Pelletier

An obscure rose (date and origin unknown) still in cultivation at Mottisfont Abbey and Roseraie de l'Haÿ, possibly developed at the latter. Very double, mid-size, cerise and mauve blossoms on a medium shrub.

Fornarina

('Belle Flore' [#2])
Vétillard, France, 1826

Mid-sized, doubled, and cupped blossoms of rich rose-purple, more deeply colored at the centers and spotted with blush white. Vigorous upright growth to 4 feet. (1,4)

Francis Foucquier

('François Foucquier')

Not widely available and with only tentative identification, this is yet another Gallica for which details of date and origin are lost. Vivid cerise-crimson blossoms. The wavy petals are edged and spotted with the palest pink. Blooms are semi-double, each with a center of gold stamens. Rich green foliage with olive overtones. A striking and handsome specimen.

Gazelle

Before 1848

Origin unknown. Very large, delicate, pink blossoms. (1)

Général Moreau

Date and origin unknown. Listed by Trevor Griffiths, this carmine-purple Gallica dates from before 1906.

GEORGES VIBERT

Georges Vibert

Robert, France, 1853

Small, tight, crimson buds open to fragrant, loosely double blossoms that are clearly striped soft pale pink, muted purple-crimson, and white. The petals are recurved around the center of gold stamens, giving the blossoms an overall shaggy casual look. Growth is compact; the foliage is rich dark green.

Gil Blas

France, before 1848

Large, double, rose-crimson blossoms on a medium shrub. Possibly developed at l'Haÿ.

Named after a novel by Alain René Le Sage, French dramatist and novelist (1688-1747). (1,4,6)

Gloire de France

('Glory de France')

The rose in commerce today under this name does seem to be correctly identified but it should not be confused with 'Fanny Bias', and its name should not be given as a synonym for that rose. It is a separate rose according to historical texts. (In most rose literature, a date of 1819 is given for the Gallica 'Fanny Bias'; the 1828 date for 'Gloire de France' has been established by Graham Stuart Thomas.) Most likely a Gallica-Centifolia hybrid, 'Gloire de France' grows vigorously and quickly forms a thicket, but its canes spread and arch under the weight of profuse bloom. Furthermore, it has soft matte green foliage that is not particularly Gallica in character. (See discussion under 'Fanny Bias'.)

The blossoms, doubled and informally quartered, have rich cerise-rose centers with soft pink borders, paling with age to lilac tones. 'Gloire de France' is a well-formed shrub, which quickly establishes in almost any location. Even when planted in partially shaded areas, it will put forth a glorious profusion of bloom. (1)

Gloire des Jardins

Descemet, France, before 1834

Dramatic deep purple-crimson, fragrant flowers, doubled and cupped, with a small center of bunched gold stamens. The incurved petals are silvery on the reverse. Mid-sized blossoms on a medium shrub.

Gloriette

Robert, France, before 1848

A Gallica-China hybrid. Abundant, very pretty blossoms, quite double. Small yellow eye. The outer petals are reflexed and colored pale blush pink; the inner petals are slightly cupped and stained with a darker rose color. Almost crinkled in appearance, the foliage is deeply veined. (2)

Gonsalve

France, before 1848

Mid-size, double, globular blossoms of violet-crimson. Origin uncertain, possibly developed at Roseraie de l'Haÿ where it remains in cultivation today.

Grand Cramoisi
Vibert, France, 1818

Profuse bloom of double crimson flowers. (1,4)

Grande et Belle [#1]
Before 1813

The origin of this clear rose-pink Gallica, which grew in Joséphine's collection, is unknown. (1)

Grande Renoncule

Date and origin unknown. Very double ranunculus-like blossoms of rose-pink. Not to be confused with the Centifolia, 'Grande Renoncule Violacée'. (1,7)

Grand Sultan
Before 1848

Large, very doubled, expanded purple flowers, shaded crimson. Robust growth. (1)

Gros Provins Panaché
Fontaine, France, 1860

Possibly a Gallica-China hybrid. Striking, large, doubled and quartered, well-scented blooms. The purplish rose blossoms are splashed with white. A vigorous shrub to 5 feet. (1,6)

Grosse Cerise
Van Houtte, Holland, 1843

Predictably, a large, cerise-pink Gallica. (1)

Haddington

The date and origin of this old garden rose are lost. Small to mid-size, semi-double blooms of dark purple-crimson with centers of gold stamens. Vigorous, large growth. (4)

Hector
Parmentier, Belgium, 1830

Small pomponlike (many petaled) blossoms. Violet, mauve, and rose hues, delicately striped with white. (The Homeric Trojan hero.) (1,4)

Helvetia
('Aurore', 'Aurore Helvetia')
Laffay, France, date unknown

A Gallica-China hybrid. Large, cupped, and doubled blossoms of bright crimson tinged with mauve. 'Aurore' appears to have been an alternate historical name for this rose. (2)

Henriette

The date and origin of this light clear pink Gallica with double blossoms are unknown. Grown at Malmaison. (1)

Henri Fouquier
('Henri Foucquier')
France, 1854

Large, fragrant flowers are very doubled and flattened. Petals reflex around a small button eye. The color is clear pink, aging to lilac-pink. Somewhat spreading growth with dark green foliage and nearly thornless canes. Henri Foucquier (1838-1901) was a politician and writer. (2,5,6)

Hippolyte
('Souvenir de Kean')
Early 1800's

Clusters of fragrant double flowers of deep wine red, dusted with deeper purplish shading. Color is more intense when 'Hippolyte' is grown in a semi-shaded location. At first the blooms are globular then petals reflex around the button eyes. Arching, somewhat procumbent growth (to 5 feet) and nearly thornless canes. Origin of this attractive rose is lost in the mists of history.

Kean was a well-known English actor; from classical mythology, Hippolyte was an Amazon queen.

HIPPOLYTE

67

HYPATHIA

Hortense de Beauharnais
Prévost, France, before 1848

Large double flowers tightly packed with petals. The blossom is rose-lilac with a rose-pink circumference. Vigorous upright growth. Named after Eugenie Hortense de Beauharnais who was the wife of Louis Bonaparte (1778-1846), king of Holland and brother of Napoléon I. (1)

Hypathia
('Hypatia', 'Hypacia')
Before 1846

Showy, fragrant, semi-double, rosy crimson flowers veined and spotted with white. Cupped form with a bold center of golden stamens. Dark green foliage and branching growth. Perhaps a Gallica-Centifolia hybrid. (1,6)

Incomparable
Before 1813

Details of origin unknown. Large, double, light rose blossoms. Listed in Joséphine's collection at Malmaison. (1)

Invincible
Miellez, France, 1836

Mid-size, bright crimson, double blossoms on a large shrub. Interestingly, 'Invincible' was listed among other "Rejected and Superseded" roses in the exhaustive 1846 catalog of William Prince. The offering warned, "Being inferior and some being synonymes. Those who desire these kinds, can have them at 18 to 25 cents each during the present season, after which they will be entirely thrown aside." As if living up to its name, this rose survives today and is grown at Sangerhausen.

Ipsilanté
('Ypsilante')
Vibert, France, 1821

A robust shrub, sprawling to 4½ feet, with sparse reddish thorns and dark green foliage. The sweetly scented flowers are lovely: lush and uncharacteristically large, doubled and swirled into irregular quarters. The color is a soft mauve-pink with paler petals at the circumference. 'Ipsilanté' flowers slightly later than most other Gallicas. It was perhaps named after the Greek patriot and general, Prince Alexander Ypsilante (1792–1828).

IPSILANTÉ

JAMES MASON

James Mason

Beales, England, 1982

'James Mason' boasts large, barely semi-double, glowing scarlet-crimson velvety flowers, each with a large boss of gold stamens at the center. Created from a cross of 'Scharlachglut' and 'Tuscany Superb', this rose has petals that are reminiscent of both parents. [See individual entries for parents.] Blossoms are scented. Dark green foliage. Vigorous yet very manageable upright growth to 5 feet. (For those in decades future who might wonder, Mr. Mason was an English actor.)

JENNY DUVAL

Jeanne Hachette

Vibert, France, 1842

Very large and full flowers of scarlet-crimson heavily spotted with bright red. (1)

Jeannette

Descemet, France, 1815

Mid-sized, doubled crimson blooms that fade to light rose. Fragrant. Vigorous strong growth. (2)

Jenny Duval

('Jenny')
Duval, France, before 1836

Claimed by some to be the same as 'Président de Sèze'; however, when correctly identified, these are two distinct roses.

The half-opened buds of 'Jenny Duval' are particularly lovely. These become large, loosely double blossoms with large wavy iridescent petals, each with a center of deep yellow stamens. The blossom color—changing with age and temperature—may appear as rose-pink violet, lavender, or mauve-gray, so that no two flowers ever seem quite the same. A charming chameleon! A strong perfume. Foliage is a lively deep green. Growth is upright but the canes may bow or arch under the weight of the flowers. The canes have uneven thorns, some thorns being quite large. Possibly a Gallica-China hybrid.

Josephina

Savoureux, France, before 1813

Large, very full blossoms of deep rose-pink. In Joséphine's collection at Malmaison. (1)

Joséphine Parmentier

Parmentier, Belgium, 1840

Mid-sized, doubled blossoms of a pretty clear pink. (2)

Juanita

Vibert, France, before 1834

A profusion of fragrant, mid-size, double blossoms of rose-pink sprinkled with white dots. Moderate, branching growth. (2)

Julie d'Estanges

France, before 1848

A Gallica hybrid with some Alba characteristics. Large, doubled and cupped, rose-lilac flowers with blush pink outer petals. Vigorous, upright growth. Now in cultivation at Roseraie de l'Haÿ where it was possibly developed.

JULIETTE

Juliette

Miellez, France, 1860

Mid-size, showy, double, carmine blooms on a large shrub. Spelling occasionally as *Julette*. (1,3,4)

Juno

Laffay, France, 1847

Possibly a Gallica-China hybrid. Profuse, large, extremely full blossoms of very pale rose on a large shrub. Not to be confused with the Centifolia of the same name. (4)

Kean [#1]

Before 1846

A popular rose in its time, 'Kean' [#1] is of unknown origin. Described by William Paul, in *The Rose Garden*, as "worthy of a place in the most limited collection." Large, full, well-formed, vivid purple-crimson blossoms with a crimson center on a vigorous branching shrub. (4)

La Belle Sultane

('Violacea', 'Gallica Maheka')
Known since late 1700's

A tall shrub—to 5 or 6 feet—with long canes and reddish bristles. Flattened, almost single flowers, each with a prominent center of gold stamens. The fragrant blossoms open velvety purple-crimson, often dusted with darker tones, and the petals pale to almost white at the base. As the bloom matures, the color turns to soft purple and brownish violet. Cane length as well as the character of the calyx and leaves of 'La Belle Sultane' have caused the speculations of possible Damask or Centifolia influence.

Today 'Violacea' and 'Gallica Maheka' are the most common synonyms for this lovely rose. Yet, through the years, other names have also swirled around it, causing additional confusion. As that of so many old roses, the history of 'La Belle Sultane' is filled with multiple names, identification problems, changing horticultural fashions, and myths.

'La Belle Sultane' originated as a European garden rose, perhaps, from Holland. Dr. Grimm of Germany has called attention to a possible early mention of this rose as either "#24 *R. provincialis flore pleno atropurpurea, holoserico*," or "#38 *R. provincialis flore holoserico atrorubente*" in the 1720 plant list for the Leyden Garden of Haarlem. German scholars have found a rose that closely resembles 'La Belle Sultane' in a 1795 illustration entitled "*Holosericea Flore Semi-Plena*." (1993 yearbook of the German Rose Society.) According to Graham Thomas (*The Old Shrub Roses*), the early nineteenth-century illustration of *Rosa holosericea duplex* (Roessig, Plate 16) shows a more petaled form of this rose.

In the 1790's, Andre Dupont imported this rose to France.

Dupont, the chief horticulturist at Malmaison who was so instrumental in obtaining roses from around the world for Joséphine's collection, would have certainly included his own import. And, indeed, 'La Belle Sultane' was on Jules Gravereaux's 1912 list of Joséphine's roses at Malmaison. All this weakens the report that Dupont distributed this rose under the English name 'Fair Sultane'.

There may have been a 'Fair Sultane' as there certainly were several 'Grande Sultane's. The synonym 'Cumberland' belongs not to 'La Belle Sultane' but to 'Grande Sultane' [#2], a more lightly colored Gallica-Centifolia hybrid from Prévost. (See index.)

A wonderful tale of this rose name, filled with all things romantic, follows: Joséphine's childhood friend in Martinique, Aimée du Buc de Rivery, was captured by Barbary pirates, taken to Algiers, and later bestowed to Sultan Selim III. On becoming a member of his harem, she was named "La Sultane Validée." This rose was supposedly named for her. Be it myth or not, the story is entirely fitting, given the interest in the Middle East during the era. And the tale does explain why yet another rose grown at Malmaison, 'Rose du Sérail' (meaning "Rose of the Harem") is sometimes added to the confusion. Remaining in cultivation today, 'Rose du Sérail' is a separate rose.

One must wonder if the second meaning in French for *sultane* is actually the more germane: "scent-sachet." This definition would explain the number of Gallica roses with *sultane* names.

Might this definition also be linked to *Maheka*? A nurseryman in Holland kindly informed me that in Urdu, a language used by Moslems on the subcontinent of India and one which sprang from Persian, *Mahak* indicates superior fragrance. (Unfortunately, I cannot substantiate an equivalent Persian word.) However, this possible linguistic link recalls Opoix's history of Provins: the town's residents boasted that their medicinal conserve made from Gallica roses had been sold as far as India by the end of the seventeenth century. The botanical origin of the term was sent to me from the Royal Horticultural Society's assistant librarian, Miss Vine: the word is actually "makeka," first cited by Heinrich Reichenback in *Flora Germanica excursoria* no. 622. The term, now invalid, was most frequently used in the rose literature of the early 1830's and was dropped by the late 1840's.

Lastly, to add a final note of confusion to this already confusing rose, the name 'Maheka' has also been associated with *R. pendulina* (or Alpina) hybrids.

There is only one 'La Belle Sultane'. Its burst of early bloom brings delight to any garden and is truly "La Belle."

La Louise
Parmentier, Belgium, 1840

Fragrant semi-double flowers of purple-crimson, each with a center of yellow stamens. The petals pale at the base to almost white. This rose is similar in appearance to 'La Belle Sultane'. (4)

La Maculée
Dupont, France, 1810

Large semi-double blossoms striped pink, purple, and crimson on a large shrub with slender well-armed canes. Although not the most refined, this variety—a good seed bearer—was widely used as a parent to produce the spotted and the streaked Gallicas. Grown at Malmaison. (4,6)

LA BELLE SULTANE

La Nationale

Before 1834

Origin unknown. Vivid rose-pink, large full blooms, striped and marbled with crimson. Paler at the circumference. Upright growth on a large shrub. According to Paul, the same as 'Nationale Tricolore'. (See index.) (4)

La Neige

Robert, France, 1853

Imagine a small snowball beginning to roll from the top a hill, slowly it grows bigger and bigger. An apt description of the confusion surrounding this obscure hybrid rose of unknown origin. Distinct from the Moss rose by the same name, 'La Neige' is among the very few white Gallicas. Fragrant and double, white with a touch of green. However, this rose is possibly the same as a pre-1838 Gallica-Centifolia hybrid, 'Boule de Neige' [#2] ('Globe White Hip'). (See index.) And, yes, that rose—be it the same as 'La Neige' or not—should not be confused with a Bourbon rose (1867) also named 'Boule de Neige'.

Aside, but entirely fitting, one French dictionary defines *boule de neige* as snowball; figuratively "to grow bigger and bigger" is *faire boule de neige*. Perhaps, there was a premonition when this rose was named. (6)

La Plus Belle des Ponctuées

Mme. Hébert, France, 1829

Large, loosely full flowers of a rich rose-pink color, finely spotted with paler pink and perfumed with a fine fragrance. Bright green foliage. Tall growth up to 6 feet. The origin and date of this rose are cited by James Russell in *Old Garden Roses*, Part II. *Ponctuée* means "spotted." (4,5,6)

La Roxelane

Vibert, France, 1828

A violet-colored Gallica. (1,5)

La Tendresse

('Rose Tendre')
Before 1834

Origin unknown. A light rose-pink Gallica in cultivation at Roseraie de l'Haÿ.

Ledonneau-Leblanc

Origin and date unknown. A large, double white flower with blush shadings. Vigorous growth and dark green foliage. (4)

L'Enchanteresse

('Enchantresse', 'Grande Henriette')
Belgium, 1826

Large, double blossoms. Evenly colored, pale clear pink, and touched with lavender at the edges. The flowers are cupped, beautifully formed, and abundantly produced. Upright moderate growth. Although a Gallica-Centifolia hybrid, this rose presents a greater number of Gallica characteristics. (1,4,6,7)

Le Phoenix

Vibert, France, 1843

Large carmine and pink, very double, fragrant blossoms on a large shrub. Not to be confused with 'Phénix'/'Phoenix'. See entry. (4)

Les Saisons d'Italie

Date and origin are unknown for this Gallica currently in cultivation at Sangerhausen. Vivid purple-crimson, mid-size, very double blossoms with a heavy fragrance. A large shrub. (Could this be 'Quatre Saisons d'Italie'? See entry.)

'L'Évêque. See 'The Bishop'.

L'Ingénue

Before 1846

A Gallica-Centifolia hybrid. Mid-sized, doubled, and cupped flowers. Creamy white with a more deeply colored center. Pale green foliage and branching growth. (9)

Louis Philippe [#1]

('Grandissima')
Hardy, France, 1824

Well-perfumed and beautifully formed, the quartered blossoms of 'Louis Philippe' [#1] are very large and double. Rosy crimson with purple overtones and deeper shading around the small center of gold stamens. Spreading, branching growth to 5 feet. There is a China by the same name. (1,2,4,5,6)

Louis van Tyle

('Louis van Till', 'Louis van Tyll')

An obscure Gallica of unknown origin but still in commerce today. Crimson. Not to be confused with the Moss rose by the same name. (1,6)

Lucile Duplessis

Vibert, France, 1836

Medium-sized, doubled flowers of rich rose-pink, spotted deep rose. (1)

Lustré d'Église

('Grand St. Francis')
Before 1813

Origin unknown. Small, double, pink blooms on a mid-sized shrub. Well-perfumed. Formerly in Joséphine's collection at Malmaison and now in cultivation at Sangerhausen.

Mme. d'Hébray

Pradel, France, 1820

Large, well-formed, loosely doubled, nicely perfumed blossoms. Predominantly white with stripes of rose and crimson-pink. Small center of gold stamens. Pradel's later rose by the same name is a Centifolia. (4)

Mme. Ville

Another obscure Gallica. Attractive, mid-size, fragrant flowers of vivid purplish rose. Upright growth habit. (2)

Madelon Friquet

('Madelon Frequet')
Vibert, France, 1830

Large, beautifully formed, doubled blooms of rich clear lilac-crimson, finely spotted with blush. (2)

Majestueuse

Guerrapain, France, 1811

Large, doubled and cupped, strongly colored rose-pink blossoms on a branching and vigorous shrub. 'Majestueuse' was grown at Malmaison and remains in cultivation today at Roseraie de l'Haÿ.

This rose is either a Gallica x Bourbon or a Gallica x China hybrid (terms which were sometimes interchanged in the old listings).

Malesherbes

Vibert, France, 1834

Very large, double purple-crimson blossoms, spotted with crimson. Vigorous growth. (1,4)

Malton

Guerin, France, 1829

A Gallica-China hybrid that was important in the development of the early Hybrid Perpetuals. Brilliant velvety crimson blossoms, doubled, cupped, and globular in form. Vigorous, branching yet spreading growth with dense attractive red-tinged foliage. (1)

Manteau Pourpre

Vibert, France, 1823

Mid-size, velvety purple-crimson, double blossoms on a medium-sized shrub. (1,4)

Manteau Royal

Descemet, France, 1810

Intensely colored flowers: velvet-like, vivid crimson flowers with touches of bright purple. The double blossoms of 'Manteau Royal' are medium-sized and have slightly quilled petals, providing a glimpse of gold stamens at the center of each. (2)

Marcel Bourgoin

('Le Jacobin')
Corboeuf-Marsault, France, 1899

Loosely doubled and somewhat muddled blossom with yellow stamens visible at the center. The rich velvety reddish purple bloom ages to dusky violet. The reverse of the petals is a much paler shade. Small, rich green leaves and erect growth habit. (2,5,9)

Marie Antoinette

Vibert, France, 1825

Lilac-crimson, large, double flowers. At first cupped, the bloom then opens into a beautifully quartered blossom with a small yellow eye. Vigorous healthy growth. (4)

Marie Tudor

l'Haÿ, France, date unknown

Cherry-crimson and salmon-pink mottled blossoms. (1,4)

Mazeppa

('Mazzeppa')
Before 1846

The origin of this interesting old garden rose is unknown. Loosely double, irregular blooms, somewhat ragged in appearance. Bright crimson-pink, edged and marbled in white. Golden button eye. Bright green, deeply veined foliage. (Lord Bryon's poem by the same name is about a Polish nobleman.)

Mécène

Vibert, France, 1845

A double, white rose striped with lilac-pink. Nearly thornless canes and moderate erect growth. (1,2,3,4,6)

Mercedes

Vibert, France, 1847

Large full blossoms of lilac-pink and white that pale to blush and white. (1)

Moïse [#1]

Parmentier, Belgium, 1828

Large, very full, and expanded blossoms of crimson, shaded purple and mauve-gray. Erect growth habit. (1,4,6)

Montalembert

Moreau and Robert, France, 1852

A dark lilac-colored Gallica. (1,2)

Montezuma

Coquerel, France, circa 1906

This Gallica has lilac-pink blossoms with a paler circumference. (1)

Montigny

Date and origin unknown. A crimson Gallica in the collection at Roseraie de l'Haÿ, possibly developed there.

Nanette

Prior to 1848

Blooming later than most other Gallicas, 'Nanette' has clusters of small, neat, deeply rose-colored blossoms, veined and marbled with purple-crimson. Each bloom, cupped and doubled, has a small button eye. Growth habit is small and compact. Dark green foliage. (2,5,6)

Napoléon

('Souvenir des Français')
Hardy, France, before 1834

Developed by the Superintendent of the Luxembourg Gardens in Paris, this shrub features unusually large, double flowers of vivid rose that are dusted with purple. The petals are large and thick. Growth is upright and vigorous with attractive foliage. This is another rose that has successfully battled changing tastes. Rejected, superseded, and tossed onto the bargain table by William Prince in 1846, 'Napoléon' survives in cultivation today.

Whenever I find a Gallica by this name, I immediately recall Samual Parson's lament, "Any half-dozen English or French rose growers may give the name of their favorite Wellington or Napoleon to a rose raised by each of them, and entirely different in form and color from the other five bearing the same name. Thus has arisen the great confusion in rose nomenclature."

Narcisse de Salvandy

Van Houtte, Holland, 1843

Clusters of large, flat, double blooms, each with a big boss of yellow stamens. Rich cerise-rose. Spreading growth. (1,4,6)

Néala

Vibert, France, 1822

Mid-sized, doubled blooms of rich rose-carmine with paler petals at the circumference. (1)

Néron

('Nero')

Laffay, France, 1841

Rich violet-crimson flowers, doubled and with more deeply colored centers. The medium, very full blooms are spotted chocolate, and the dappling darkens with age. Reflexing petals. Vigorous branching growth to 5 feet. Gallica-Centifolia hybrid. (1,4,5)

Nestor

France

Details of origin are uncertain. Possibly by Laffay, circa 1841. Beautifully formed, marvelously perfumed blossoms. Cupped at first then reflexed with a neatly quartered center where the lilac-rose color of 'Nestor' deepens. Fades to mauve-pink with age. Rich green foliage and nearly thornless canes. (Nestor, son of Chloris, was the wisest man in Homer's *Iliad*) Be wise and place this rose in your garden; in mine, it is one of my most appreciated roses. Hardly just another pink! A lovely rose. (5)

NESTOR

News

LeGrice, England, 1968

This recent Gallica hybrid was produced by a cross of 'Tuscany Superb' [See entry.] and the Floribunda 'Lilac Charm'. The resulting blossoms are semi-double with thick petals of deep rich purple-crimson, each with a handsome center of gold stamens. Dark olive green, somewhat glossy foliage on a compact upright shrub reaching 2½ feet.

Nouveau Intelligible

Robert, France, 1841

A Gallica with violet-colored flowers. (1)

Nouveau Monde

Descemet, France

Still another obscure Gallica with purple-violet blossoms in cultivation at Roseraie de l'Haÿ.

Nouveau Vulcain

France, 1820

Mid-size double blooms of dark rich purple with violet tones. (1,4,5)

Nouvelle Pivoine

Origin and date unknown. Possibly developed at Roseraie de l'Haÿ. Large violet-crimson blossoms with centers of vivid crimson. (1)

Nouvelle Transparente

Miellez, France, 1833

Large, bright rose-crimson, double flowers. Strongly perfumed. (1)

Octavie [#1]

Coquerel, France, 1800

Mid-sized, doubled, and expanded blooms of light rose, edged blush pink. Vigorous branching growth. See index for two other roses that were given this name. (Wife of Marc Antony.) (1)

Oeillet Double

Prévost, France, 1829

A Gallica with lilac-pink carnation-like blossoms. (*Oeillet* refers to the flower shape of dianthus or pinks.) Both Dutch and French hybridizers commonly described roses by comparing them with other flowers. (1)

Oeillet Flamand

Vibert, France, 1845

Very doubled, expanded and somewhat flattened, mid-sized blossoms. These are produced in small clusters atop erect flower stalks. The ground color is rose, dappled with pale lilac-rose. Dark green foliage. Red-tinged new growth. William Paul wrote of this rose: "A very desirable variety, producing its flowers more frequently true in character than the general run of Striped Roses."

Oeillet Flamand

OEILLET PARFAIT

OFFICINALIS

84

Oeillet Parfait

Foulard, France, 1841

Clusters of fragrant pale blush to white, doubled and flattened flowers, striped bright lilac rose-crimson. (1,3,4,5,6)

Officinalis

(Apothecary's Rose, Rose of Provins, Red Rose of Lancaster, *R. gallica maxima*, *R. g. duplex*)

Rosa gallica 'Officinalis', an ancestor of many modern roses, is quite possibly the oldest rose to be cultivated in European gardens.

A charming, simple, and tenacious rose, it remains growing around old foundations centuries after being planted. 'Officinalis' is a survivor. Its semi-double blossom consists of approximately four rows of petals, bright crimson to violet-crimson, arranged around a prominent center of gold stamens. The fragrance is intense and lingers in its dried petals; this trait earned the Rose of Provins its highly important place within the centuries-old apothecary trade and further insured its survival. Today, gardeners continue to enjoy the simple beauty and wonderful scent of this historic rose. See introductory chapters for additional comments.

Ohl

Vibert, France, 1830

The well-perfumed blossoms are large, full, violet-purple. Slight marbling and centers of rich crimson. Vigorous branching growth with deep green foliage and few thorns. (1,4,5)

Ombrée Parfaite

('Ombrée Parfait', 'Purple-Variegated Provins Rose') Vibert, France, 1823

Double, mid-size, fragrant blooms in clusters of various shades from soft pink to violet-purple, sometimes in the same flower. Definitely, a "Mad Gallica." Compact growth to 3 feet. (2,4,5, 6,8)

Ombre Panachée

Before 1813

Few details are known about this Gallica that was once grown in Joséphine's collection. Full, velvety crimson-purple blossoms. (1)

Ombre Superbe

Before 1813

Dark velvety blackish purple, double blossoms. Most details of origin for this dark and lovely Gallica are lost. It was grown in Joséphine's collection at Malmaison. (1)

Omphale
Vibert, France, 1845

Large blossoms, doubled. A particularly lovely clear rose-pink that is occasionally spotted with white. Upright growth. This rose bears the name from classical tales of the Queen of Lydia with whom Heracles spent three years. (1)

Onex

Golden yellow stamens grace the center of the semi-double, symmetrically round blossoms. Purple to violet. Well-foliated 'Onex' is of average height and spread. Available through German and Dutch nurseries.

Ornement de la Nature
('Anémone Ancienne', 'Rose Anémone')
Godefroy, France, 1826

Beautifully formed, very doubled and quartered, mid-sized blossoms. The color is soft lilac-rose, tinged with a darker hue. Tall-growing shrub. (1)

Orpheline de Juillet
('Orpheline Juillet')
Before 1837

Abundant bloom of large, very double flowers with petals neatly and tightly arranged. Deep rich crimson-purple with vivid crimson coloring at the base of the petals and sometimes streaking outward into the petals. A somewhat sprawling and thorny shrub. (2)

Palais de Laeken
1824

Origin unknown and the Gallica heritage possibly limited. Mid-size, vivid pink, double blossoms, shaded with deeper and brighter tones. A large shrub. Named after and possibly originating at the Laeken estate (main residence of the King of Belgium), known for its extensive gardens. (4)

Pallas
Guerrapin, France, 1811

A crimson Gallica which was in Joséphine's collection at Malmaison. (Another name for the Greek goddess Athena.) (1)

OMPHALE

Panachée d'Angers

('Commandant Beaurepaire')
Moreau and Robert, France, 1879

A Hybrid Perpetual among the Gallicas? 'Panachée d'Angers' is included here for the perspective that its story brings to rose history, marketing, and classification.

Originally classed as a Gallica under the name 'Commandant Beaurepaire', it began as an unknown hybrid. However, when this rose was discovered to be reblooming, it was renamed 'Panachée d'Angers' and listed with the far more marketable Hybrid Perpetuals. By the 1870's, after all, Gallicas were old news! Only a fine line separates this rose from the Gallicas: the Gallica designation still persists in various texts and listings. The collection lists of both Sangerhausen and Roseraie de l'Haÿ continue to designate it as a Gallica. Interesting comments on this rose are found in Dickerson's *Old Rose Advisor*.

The cupped blossoms of 'Panachée d'Angers' are large, double, and rich pink, striped purple and lilac and spotted with white.

Panachée Superbe [#2]

Laffay, France, 1841

Double crimson blossoms. (1)

Paquita

Before 1838

Origin unknown. Large, double, violet-rose blossoms. (1)

Park Wilhelmshöhe

Kordes, Germany, 1987

A modern Gallica hybrid. Dense growth with slightly glossy rich green foliage. Loosely double, carmine-rose blossoms, each with a center of gold stamens. Named for the fabled rose garden in Kassel, Germany.

Passe Princesse

('De La Reine', 'Grand Royale', 'Grandesse Royale',
'Grandeur Royale', 'Rose Pivone')
Dupont, France, before 1813

Very large, full blossoms of purple-rose, paling to lilac-rose. Branching growth. In Joséphine's collection at Malmaison. Godefroy and Prévost are also associated with this rose, thus indicating that either additional names were given by the various nurserymen or several of the names are shared by different roses. (1)

Passe Velours

('Nouvelle Maheca','Beauvelours', 'Grande Obscurité')
Descemet, France, before 1813

Mid-size, semi-double blossoms. Rich dark velvety purple with brown undertones. In Joséphine's collection at Malmaison. See index for discussion of 'Maheca Nova'. (1)

Pepita

Moreau, France

Date unknown. Double blossoms of soft rose-pink with white stripes. (1)

Perle des Panachées

('Cottage Maid')
Vibert, France, 1845

William Paul's praise for this rose in *The Rose Garden* is as true today as it was in 1848: "One of the best striped Roses." Mid-sized, doubled and expanded, wonderfully scented blossoms. The pale blush to white blooms are distinctly striped with deep rose-pink. 'Perle des Panachées' is a compact tidy shrub, 3 feet. Bright green foliage and fine reddish prickles. See discussion under 'Village Maid'. (1)

Perle von Weissenstein

('Pearl of Weisenstein', 'Perle de Veissenstein',
'La Négresse')
Schwarzkopf, Germany, 1773

Dusky mauve blossoms with a deeper purplish center. The name refers to the early garden in Kassel, Germany. On introduction into France, the rose was renamed 'La Négresse'. (1,4)

Pérou de Gossart

Possibly developed at Roseraie de l'Haÿ, date unknown. Cerise-pink blossoms, shaded vivid crimson. (4)

Petite Orléanaise

('Petite Orléannaise')
France, 1845

An early flowering Gallica. Large clusters of mid-size blossoms, each neatly well-formed bloom with a center of incurved petals and a tight boss of gold stamens. Color is uniformly bright rose-crimson. The flowers are strongly fragrant. Bright green foliage and tall growth to 4½ feet. (1)

Pharericus

('Wariricus')

Date and origin unrecorded. Medium to large, full, compact, well-formed, light but bright rose-pink blossoms, shaded mauve. Profuse bloom and upright growth. (4)

Phénix

('Phoenix, 'Lyre de Flore', 'Panachée Superbe' [#1])
Hardy, France, 1823

A small, double, pink Gallica currently in cultivation at Sanger-hausen where the identification is tentative. Early blooming with a strong fragrance. Listed as grown at Malmaison; therefore, possibly of an earlier date.

Pluton [#2]

('Rose Pluton', possibly 'Pluto')
Vibert, France, 1843

Medium-sized blossoms, doubled and cupped. The color of 'Pluton' [#2] is deep rich violet-purple with a darker blush. Branching growth. This is perhaps the same rose as the similarly described 'Pluto' in Prince's *Manual of Roses*. (1)

Pompon Panachée

('Pompon de Panachée', 'Pompon' [#2])
Robert and Moreau, France, 1858

Flattened and doubled flowers of creamy white, tinged green and splashed with pink and lilac, fading to white and pale pink. Small leaves, thin canes. Short dense growth to 3 feet. (6)

Ponctuée

Madame Hébert, France, 1829

A Gallica with spotted rose-pink blossoms. (1)

Perle des Panachées

Portland Rose

('Duchess of Portland', *Rosa* x *portlandica*,
'Scarlet Four Seasons')

Quite Gallica-like in appearance yet reblooming, this rose is possibly a Gallica ('Officinalis'?) hybrid with *R. damascena bifera*. Semi-double, bright cerise-crimson, fragrant blossoms, each with a large boss of gold stamens. I always appreciate this rose in the late garden for its old-fashioned form and fragrance.

Much debate encircles this rose, its origin and history. The name, 'Duchess of Portland', refers to the second Duchess of Portland (1715-1785), an English rose enthusiast, who reportedly brought the rose from Italy. Brent Dickinson's discussion of this rose in *The Old Rose Advisor* cites its mention in 1775 as the 'Portland Crimson Monthly Rose', "readily found" at that time. This rose is pivotal to hybridization of later roses as well as to the development of the Portland group of roses.

Pourpre Ardoisé

Dupont, France, before 1813

Large, double, slate-purple blossoms. In Joséphine's collection.

Pourpre Charmant

('Rouge Admirable' [#1], 'La Magnifique',
'Grand Pompadour', 'Regulus')
Dupont, France

Large, vivid, velvety-purple, semi-double blossoms. A handsome rose on a medium to tall shrub. Listed in Joséphine's collection at Malmaison and grown today at Roseraie de l'Haÿ.

Président de Sèze

('Mme. Hébert')
Hébert, France, 1836

This strong-growing, arching shrub (to 4½ feet) is adorned with a profusion of blossoms in clusters. The double flowers are beautifully formed, cupped at first, opening to quartered and flattened blooms. The outer recurved petals are pale lilac-rose, veined with a darker hue; the centers are a rich mauve-crimson, each punctuated by a knot of gold stamens. See discussion under 'Jenny Duval'.

Président Dutailley

('Charlemagne')
Dubreuil, France, 1888

Raised from open-pollinated seed from a Gallica parent, this curious hybrid was originally classified by Dubreuil as a "Reblooming Gallica." Clusters of 3 to 4 large blossoms, heavily perfumed and well formed. At first the bloom is cupped and slightly quartered around a tiny boss of yellow stamens; with age the outer petals recurve. The color is bright lilac-crimson with carmine shadings. Matte green foliage and vigorous growth. The strong canes are well armed with thorns and bristles. (1,2,4,7)

Prince Frédéric

Parmentier, Belgium, 1840

Large, very double, fragrant, brilliant crimson flowers on a tall shrub. (4,6)

Princesse de Nassau

Miellez, France

A rose with dark pink blossoms. This is different from the late-summer blooming rose mentioned in *Graham Stuart Thomas' Rose Book* as possibly being the same as "Mrs. Gore's 'Princesse de Nassau' of 1897." (1)

Provins Ancien

Cochet, France

Date unknown. A clear light pink Gallica. (1)

Provins Marbré

An obscure pink Gallica, reputedly grown in Joséphine's garden, currently in cultivation at Roseraie de l'Haÿ.

Provins Renoncule

('Agathe Renoncule', 'Renoncule')
Dupont, France, before 1813

Small, very double, pale pink blossoms, well formed. Grown in Joséphine's collection at Malmaison. The Ranunculus roses were once prized for their unusual form, but by the early 1840's the old *Ranunculus* rose was already placed on Prince's "Rejected" list. As the larger exhibition-type blooms became more popular, the old curiosities faded. (1,7)

Pucelle de Lille

Miellez, France, 1860

Deep rich pink, large, double blossoms on an upright mid-sized shrub. According to Trevor Griffiths, 'Pucelle de Lille' was a widely grown, well-regarded variety at one time. (4)

Quatre Saisons

(*R. damascena bifera* hort., *R. d. semperflorens*, *R. bifera*, Autumn Damask, Rose of Paestum)

An ancient rose, perhaps the "biferi Rosaria Paesti" mentioned by Virgil circa 50 B.C. Various opinions are held regarding its parentage; the most widely held view is that this hybrid resulted from a cross of *R. gallica* and *R. moschata*. The Gallica parent is rarely questioned; the historical importance of this rose is unquestioned. Thus, the Autumn Damask is included in this volume.

Loosely double, fragrant, soft pink blossoms on a lax-growing shrub with gray-green foliage. Repeat bloom.

Quatre Saisons d'Italie
('Rosier de la Malmaison')

A crimson, double, Portland-type rose of considerable antiquity and of unrecorded parentage. This rose bears a strong resemblance to the Gallicas, as do many of the earliest Portland roses.

Produced consistently throughout the season, the extremely fragrant, light bright crimson blossoms are well formed. Taller than most Portlands, the shrub reaches 4 feet in height. Quite hardy.

'Quatre Saisons d'Italie' is thought to have been imported from Florence by Andre Dupont in 1795. (And later reintroduced by Verdier in 1865.)

Randall

Loosely doubled, well-formed, crimson-pink blooms. The blossoms resemble those of 'Alika' but have more petals. Thought to have been carried to western Canada by early pioneers. 'Randall' is less cold tolerant than 'Alika'.

Reine de Perse

Date and origin unknown. Fragrant, small, double blooms of blush pink to white on a large shrub. (4)

Reine des Amateurs
Mme. Hébert, France, 1838

Very large, clear deep lilac-pink flowers with a paler circumference. Doubled, well-shaped, and wonderfully scented. A tall-growing shrub. (1,4,6)

Renoncule Ponctuée
('Spotted Ranunculus')
Vibert, France, possibly 1825

Lightly fragrant, double, Ranunculus-like blossoms. The rose-pink blossoms are spotted blush pink and are edged with deeper cherry red. With age the petals reflex. Upright, vigorous growth on a mid-sized shrub. (4)

Robert le Diable
France, before 1850

Definitely a devil to classify. Centifolia? China? Gallica? Unquestionably a hybrid, this late-flowering rose possesses sufficient Gallica traits to gain its place here.

Its double, mid-size blooms are tinted lilac-purple, violet-purple, cerise, crimson, and gray, changing to mauve-gray at maturity. The blossoms are well formed with reflexing outer petals and incurving erect inner petals. The dark green foliage is elongated. Reaching medium height, 'Robert le Diable' sprawls.

Named after the French duke who was the father of William the Conqueror; an opera by Meyerbeer.

Roi des Pourpres
Descemet, France, 1800

Full purple blossoms, shaded crimson. Considered to be an Agathe, it is one of the few to be dark in color. (1)

Rosa Mundi
(*R. gallica* 'Versicolor')

A variegated sport of 'Officinalis' and a parent of many striped Gallica roses.

Form, size, growth, and foliage are very similar to those of 'Officinalis'. Bloom color provides the significant difference: The blush to pale rose blossoms of 'Rosa Mundi' are randomly striped and liberally splashed with crimson.

The legend of this rose tells that it was named for Fair Rosamond, the mistress of Henry II who reigned in England from 1154-1189. See introductory chapters for additional comments. Scholars debate when 'Rosa Mundi' entered our gardens; Graham Thomas has noted documentation of this rose in the old herbals of Clusius, Besler, and Bauhin, thus firmly placing "Rosamonde" in European gardens before the 1580's.

A striking rose, 'Rosa Mundi' proves that even the oldest roses can be as eye-catching as the modern creations. Beauty and history, too.

Rose de Schelfhout
('De Schelfont')
Parmentier, Belgium, 1840

Medium-sized, doubled blossoms of blush pink with a delicate but intense fragrance. Currently offered in Belgium.

Rose du Maître d'École
('Maître d'École', 'De la Maître d'École')
Miellez, France, 1840

A pretty rose with rich lilac-pink blossoms that become more deeply shaded as the blooms age. Graced with the fragrance of violets. The form is fully doubled and quartered with inner petals incurving and showing a paler reverse around a small center of gold stamens. The clusters of large blossoms are well displayed against rich green foliage.

Rosa Mundi

95

Rose du Maître d'École

Rose du Sérail

Before 1813

Catalogued as having grown in Joséphine's collection at Malmaison, the origin of this obscure Gallica is lost. *Sérail* means "harem," and this rose has sometimes been considered the same as 'La Belle Sultane' with which it shares many characteristics. However, in Gravereaux's list of the Malmaison roses, 'Rose du Sérail' and 'La Belle Sultane' were separate entries. (1)

Rose Foucheaux

('Foucheaux')

Details of date and origin are lost for this carmine Gallica, which is currently grown at Roseraie de l'Haÿ.

Rosier d'El Golea

A Gallica grown at Roseraie de l'Haÿ and apparently listed nowhere else.

Rosier des Parfumeurs

('Des Parfumeurs')
P. Cochet, France

A very old, pale pink Gallica, circa 1800, in the collection at Roseraie de l'Haÿ. A superior fragrance must be assumed.

Rouge Admirable [#2]

('Orphise' [#1])
Vibert, France, 1825

Well-formed, large, doubled blossoms of light purple or deep violet-pink. (4)

Royal Marbré

Moreau & Robert, France, 1851

Mid-sized, flattened, doubled, and quartered flowers of crimson-pink, marbled with pink. A tall shrub to 5 feet. (1,4)

Ruth

Wright, Canada, 1947

An interesting hardy rose produced by crossing 'Mary L. Evans', a non-reblooming hybrid rugosa, with 'Alika' (See entry). The resulting blossoms are double and light crimson. A once-blooming tall shrub to 7 feet.

St. Nicholas

England, 1950

A volunteer seedling, possibly a Gallica-Damask hybrid, discovered by Robert James. The semi-double blossoms of lovely soft coral-pink pale around the centers of gold stamens. Its blooms are composed of wavy petals and are loosely arranged in clusters. A small shrub (to 3 feet) with gray-green foliage and a good crop of hips.

SCHARLACHGLUT

Sanchetti

Robert, France, before 1848

Very large, doubled, cupped flowers. Uniform deep pink. William Paul praised this variety as "A noble Rose." Vigorous upright growth. (1,8)

Scharlachglut

('Scarlet Fire', 'Scarlet Glow')
Kordes, Germany, 1952

From a cross of 'Alika' (See entry.) and the Hybrid Tea 'Poinsettia'. Velvety, single, scarlet-crimson blossoms, each with a showy center of gold stamens. Opening flat then reflexing, the blossoms are well displayed against rich dark green foliage. 'Scharlachglut', an early bloomer, is a beautiful sight in full blossom. Even in partial shade, this rose maintains intense blossom color, providing a dazzling display. A tall-arching shrub to 8 feet. Orange urn-shaped hips in the fall. Its shade tolerance, growth habit, and bold color permit and encourage many garden uses.

Séguier [#2]
Robert, France, 1853

Mid-size, full, violet-purple blooms, spotted with light crimson, on a shrub of medium growth. (1,4)

Sissinghurst Castle
('Rose des Maures')

A profuse bloom of deep purple-crimson blossoms dusted with dark purple. Compact, semi-double to double flowers with bright gold stamens and good fragrance. Rich green foliage. Thin stems armed with fine red prickles on a mid-sized shrub to 3 feet.

An older Gallica reintroduced in 1947, this rose was discovered by Vita Sackville-West in the ruins that would become her garden at Sissinghurst Castle in Kent. One of the finest deep dark crimson varieties.

Soleil Brillant
('Rouge Brillant', 'Rising Sun')
Before 1813

Medium, very double blossoms of bright crimson-purple. Thornless canes. The origin of this rose, grown in Joséphine's collection at Malmaison, is unknown. (1)

SISSINGHURST CASTLE

Splendens

This name is sometimes incorrectly applied to 'Officinalis'. However, 'Splendens', reaching 6 feet, is significantly taller than 'Officinalis'. Its semi-double blossoms are bright ruby crimson. Origin and date unknown. This rose is not listed in any display garden (probably because of the name confusion), but it is still sold in Europe.

Sterkmanns

Vibert, France, 1847

Large bright crimson blooms on a mid-sized shrub. (1,4,5)

Sultana

('Maxima', 'Regina')

Origin and date unknown. Very doubled, mid-sized, strongly scented blossoms of light pink. A large shrub. (4)

Surpasse Tout

('Cerisette la Jolie')
Before 1832

Origin unknown. Large double blossoms of deep rose-cerise with a pale rose color on the reverse of the petals. At first the blossoms are cupped; later the outer petals are reflexed. Inner petals incurve around a small tight boss of yellow stamens. Strongly perfumed. A dense-growing shrub with large deep green leaves and crimson prickles.

SURPASSE TOUT

Temple d'Apollon'

('Temple of Apollo', 'Barbinegra', 'Barbe à Négre', 'Barbanigra', 'Chermesissimo Amplo', 'Cramoisissimo Amplo')
Before 1813

Large, loosely double, deep violet to crimson, shaded velvety purple.

Some confusion surrounds 'Temple d'Apollon' and its many synonyms. 1813 is cited because Gravereaux listed 'Temple d'Apollon' among those grown in Joséphine's garden. However, if the attribution to Vibert is correct, the date would be 1820. (1)

SURPASSE TOUT

THALIE LA GENTILE

THE BISHOP

Thalie la Gentile
France, 1800's

Exact details of origin and date are unknown. Very doubled, extremely full, and quartered blossoms with reflexing petals. The petals are curiously arranged on edge around a green button eye. The color is a lively rose-pink with silvery shadings. A good fragrance. Possibly a Gallica-Damask hybrid. Grown at Malmaison. (1,4)

The Bishop
('Le Rosier Évêque', 'L'Évêque')
Before 1799

Colorful and abundant bloom of double and very full flowers, bright cerise-purple fading to mauve grays with bluish tones. The well-formed blossoms consist of evenly arranged petals, which roll and reflex with age. A small tight boss of gold stamens. Growth reaches 4½ feet; the canes often bend from the weight of the blossoms. Very showy in full bloom. One of my favorite roses.

Although 'The Bishop' is sometimes classified as a Centifolia, the beautiful rose under this name today possesses few Centifolia traits. At most, possibly a Gallica-Centifolia hybrid. Its many wonderful Gallica characteristics support the suggestions of Graham Stuart Thomas and of others that 'The Bishop' is the same as the old French Gallica variety 'L'Évêque'. 'Le Rosier Évêque' was grown at Malmaison. (1)

Tricolore [#1]
('Rosa Tricolor', 'Ruban Doré', 'Belle Alliance', 'Gallica Mexica Aurantia')
Lahaye-pére, France, 1827

Vivid crimson, mottled and shaded with violet-purple. A white-colored stripe in the center of the petals. The form is doubled, full petaled, and quartered. A good fragrance. Dark green matte foliage.

See index for a number of other similarly named roses.

Tricolore de Flandre
van Houtte, Belgium, 1846

Sometimes as 'Tricolor de Flandres'. The small to mid-size, very double, fragrant blossoms are packed with short petals that are arranged around a green button eye. Palest blush to white ground color is boldly and plentifully striped and splashed with crimson-purple, aging to lilac-mauve. Small upright shrub to 3 feet with dark green foliage. A very charming little rose—so much character packed into its small blossoms!

Triomphe de Flore
('Triumph of Flora')
Prévost, France, before 1813

Very full flowers, medium sized and well formed. Delicate rose-pink, paler at the circumference. Lightly scented. Tall growth with thornless canes. Grown in Joséphine's collection at Malmaison. (1,4,6)

TRICOLORE DE FLANDRE

Turenne

Vibert, France, 1846

Bright crimson, large, double flowers shaded with deep rose. Abundant bloom and good perfume. (1)

Tuscany

(Old Velvet Rose)

Dark wine crimson, loosely double flowers with a blackish blush and showy golden stamens. The petals have a velvety texture, the bases paling to almost white. The petal's reverse side is lilac-pink. Upright growth to 3 feet and dark green foliage. A wonderfully dramatic rose. When grown in a sunny location, this is the darkest rose imaginable. I prefer this simpler and bolder rose to 'Tuscany Superb'. One of the oldest Gallicas.

The Velvet rose, described in Gerard's *The Herball or General Historie of Plantes* (1596), is very similar to 'Tuscany': "very low, like unto the red rose, having branches covered with a certain hairy or prickley matter, as fine as hairs, yet not so sharp that it will harm the most tender skin . . . the leaves are like the leaves of the white rose; the flowers grow at the top of the stalks, doubled with some yellow thrums in the middle . . . of a deep and black red color, resembling red crimson velvet, whereupon some have called it the Velvet rose." Gerard continued by describing the hips as "red berries full of hard seeds, wrapped in a down or woollinesse." Graham Thomas has noted its appearance in Andrew's *Roses* (1828) as *centifolia subnigrae*. In commenting on the darkness of its flowers, William Prince noted that this rose was also called 'Black Tuscany'.

Tuscany Superb

('Superb Tuscan')

Known since 1837, this is most likely a sport of 'Tuscany'. 'Tuscany Superb' is more vigorous and has larger foliage and fuller flowers than those of 'Tuscany'. Fewer stamens are visible.

Valence Dubois

Fontaine, France, 1880

This hybrid Gallica has mid-sized, well-formed blossoms that are double, fragrant, and pink. A shrub of moderate growth. (4)

Van Artevelde

Holland, 1820

Deep rose-colored blossoms, very double and large with petals overlapping in whorls. (4,5)

Velours Pourpre

Dupont, France, before 1813

Small to medium, double blooms of deep velvety purple-crimson. Listed by Gravereaux as in Joséphine's collection at Malmaison. (1)

Tuscany Superb

TUSCANY SUPERB

106

Velutinaeflora

('Velutiniflora', *R. g. velutinaeflora*)
Before 1872

Velvety, large, single, violet-pink, fragrant blossoms open from pointed buds. Prominent gold stamens. Gray-green dense foliage on a compact plant (to 3 feet). One of the very few single Gallicas to be variously described as crimson, pinkish purple, or light cerise! The color of the old rose under this name today is paler than that implied by many descriptions. (7)

Victor Parmentier

Origin and date unknown. The bright dusky crimson blossoms are mid-size and fragrant. Cupped in form, loosely double with a small center of yellow stamens. Discovered growing at Roseraie de l'Haÿ. (4,5)

Village Maid

('La Rubanée' [#2])
Vibert, France, 1845

The blossoms of 'Village Maid' show irregular and varied stripes of white, lilac, and light crimson. These various ribbons of color often so dominate or cover the rose that the crimson-purple ground color itself appears as stripes; hence its other name is 'La Rubanée' (or covered with ribbons). Large, doubled, and cupped blossoms.

Clearly, 'Village Maid' is among the most historically unclear of all the Gallicas. Not only is it entangled with many synonyms ('Belle Rubine', 'La Belle Villageoise', 'La Rubanée', La Villageoise', 'Panachée Double', 'Gallique Panachée'), this rose has also been confused with *R. centifolia variegata*. One must venture back into rose literature in order to untangle these various ribbons of names and roses.

In Catherine Gore's 1838 book *The Rose Fancier's Manual*, which acknowledged debt to an earlier 1836 French work by Pierre Boitard (*Manuel Complet de l'Amateur de Roses*) an early mention of what is likely the original "Village Maid" appears as 'Gallique Panachée' 'La Villageoise'. Thus dating before 1836, this rose is described as having "Flowers, semi-double, large, variegated, white, striped with deep pink or cherry-colour." Then, in William Paul's *The Rose Garden* appeared a 'New Village Maid', that was designated as having been imported from St. Frond, Belgium, in 1829, and described as more double and compact. Paul's comparison would push back the date of the first "Village Maid" to before 1829. Paul's listing is confirmed by *Noms de Roses* and its entry for 'Nouvelle Ruban. de Enghien' or the New Rubanée of Belgium. (Enghien, in Belgium, is known primarily for the seventeenth-century garden estate purchased by Prince Charles d'Arenberg.) To 'La Villageoise' or 'Gallique Panachée' is given the synonym, 'La Rubanée'. At this point, all the names swirl around only two roses, but the 'Village Maid' known today has not yet appeared, and the entanglement worsened!

A good measure of confusion appears when Prince, in 1846, added yet more synonyms: the "*Village Maid, or Panachée double, or Belle Rubine*" and the "*New Village Maid or Panachée pleine.*" To unscramble this early scramble, one must also consider several striped roses introduced by Vibert in 1839 and 1845:

1) 'Belle Villageoise', 1839, violet spotted white.
2) 'Panachée à Fleurs Pleines' or 'Panachée à Fleurs Doubles'

(a Gallica confused with 'Panachée Double' which is a Moss rose), 1839, violet and white.

3) 'Village Maid' ('La Rubanée' [#2]) introduced in 1845. Purple-crimson, streaked lilac.

4) 'Perle des Panachées (which it seems became also known as 'Cottage Maid'), 1845, white and lilac.

Nancy Steen, in *The Charm of Old Roses*, has mentioned, "Another of Vibert's roses, *R. centifolia variegata*, is commonly called 'Village Maid'—not be confused with 'Cottage Maid', a Gallica." *R. centifolia variegata*, 1845, is reputed to be a variegated sport of *R. centifolia*.

Which Gallicas do we have in cultivation now? Probably 'Village Maid' ('La Rubanée' [#2]) and 'Perle des Panachées' ('Cottage Maid'). And, precisely because so much confusion does exist, these two separate roses are likely confused within the nursery trade.

Roseraie de l'Haÿ includes both 'Village Maid' and 'Perle de Panachées' in their collection. See index for others.

Ville de Londres
('La Ville de Londres')
Robert, France, before 1848

Bright cherry crimson blossoms that are somewhat paler at the circumference. Silvery reverse of petals. Cupped with outer petals reflexing. Center of bright yellow stamens. Good fragrance and compact branching growth. Possibly a Gallica-Centifolia hybrid. (2,6)

Ville de Toulouse
Brassac, France, 1876

Fragrant blossoms with a tissuelike or translucent quality. Pale blush pink with shadings of lilac-rose in the center. The flowers are well formed and loosely doubled, with a hint of quartering. A small button eye. 'Ville de Toulouse' has medium growth with healthy rich green foliage. (1,4)

William Grant

A rose recently found in Brooks, Oregon, and named for its discoverer (who has kindly written this book's foreword without knowing of the inclusion of his namesake rose). This rose is thought to have been hybridized by the priest and rose hybridizer Father George Schoener and introduced in 1915–1917. Its original name is unknown. The foliage of 'William Grant' sufficiently resembles a Gallica to allow its placement among Gallica hybrids. The handsome pink blossoms, each with a large boss of golden stamens, are cupped and semi-doubled. Bloom is profuse on a large shrub that may also be grown as a climber. A rose well named for a dedicated rosarian.

Zoë
Miellez, France, 1810

Large, very double, fragrant pink blossoms with deeper lilac-pink near the center. Profuse bloom. Vigorous tall growth. (4)

WILLIAM GRANT

Bibliography

American Rose Society. *The American Rose Annual.* Ed. 1941 by J. H. Mc-Farland; 1948-1953 by R.C. Allen. Harrisburg, Pa. See Keays, Chandler, Bechtel, Bostock, and Johnson.

——. *Modern Roses 6:A Check-list of Rose Names Prepared in Cooperation with the International Registration Authority for Roses,* comp. in assoc. with The McFarland Co. Harrisburg, Pa.: McFarland Co., 1965.

——. *Modern Roses 8: The International Check-list of Roses.* Edited by Catherine E. Meikle. Harrisburg, Pa.: McFarland Co., 1980.

——. *Modern Roses 9:The International Checklist of Roses In Cultivation or of Historical or Botanical Importance.* Edited by P. A. Haring. Shreveport, La.:The American Rose Society, 1986.

——. *Modern Roses 10: The Comprehensive List of Roses of Historical and Botanical Importance including All Modern International Rose Registrations.* Edited by Thomas Cairns. Shreveport, La.: The American Rose Society, 1993.

Austin, David. *The Heritage of the Rose.* Woodbridge: Antique Collectors' Club, 1988.

——. *English Roses: Glorious New Roses for American Gardens.* Boston: Little, Brown & Co., 1993.

Beales, Peter. *Classic Roses.* New York: Henry Holt & Company, 1985.

Bechtel, Edwin de T. "Ancient Cultivated Roses." *The American Rose Annual* 35 (1950): 13-23.

Blunt, Wilfrid, and James Russell. *Old Garden Roses.* Part 2. London: George Rainbird, 1957.

Bostock, John, and H. T. Riley. "The Rose: Twelve Varieties of It from Pliny's *Natural History* Book XXI, Chapter 10." *The American Rose Annual* 36 (1951): 9–18.

Buist, Robert. *The Rose Manual.* Philadelphia, 1844. Reprint. New York: Earl M. Coleman, 1978.

Chandler, Josephine Craven. "Malmaison: Birthplace of Modern Roses." *The American Rose Annual* 34 (1949): 17–28.

Dickerson, Brent C. *The Old Rose Advisor.* Portland, Oreg.: Timber Press, 1992.

Dobson, Beverly, ed. and comp. *Combined Rose List.* Irvington, N.Y., 1991.

——. *Combined Rose List.* Mantua, Ohio, 1992–1994.

Doll, Wilhelm. *Der Rosen-Garten.* Leipzig: Verlagsbuchhandlung von J.J. Weber, 1855.

Fisher, John. *The Companion to Roses.* Topsfield, Mass.: Salem House Publishers, 1987.

Gerard, John, and T. Johnson. *The Herball or General Historie of Plantes.* 1633. Reprint. New York: Dover Publications, n.d.

Gordon, Jean. *Pageant of the Rose.* New York: Studio Publications in assoc. with Thomas Y. Crowell Co., 1953.

Gore, Catherine Frances. *The Book of Roses or The Rose Fancier's Manual.* London: Henry Colburn Publisher, 1836. Reprint. New York: Earl M. Coleman, 1978.

Griffiths, Trevor. *The Book of Old Roses.* 1983. Reprint. London: Michael Joseph, 1984.

——. *The Book of Classic Old Roses.* 1986. London: Michael Joseph, 1987.

——. *Celebration of Old Roses.* London: Michael Joseph, 1990.

Johnson, Mrs. Jon Otto. "The Romantic Rose." *The American Rose Annual* 33 (1948): 11–22.

Keays, Mrs. Frederick L. "Studying the Old Roses." *The American Rose Annual* 26 (1941): 5–12.

Krüssmann, Gerd. *The Complete Book of Roses.* Translated by G. K. and Nigel Raban. Portland, Oreg.: Timber Press, 1981.

Le Rougetel, Hazel. *A Heritage of Roses.* Owings Mills, Md.: Stemmer House, 1988.

List of Roses in Collection from an Austrian Castle ("Verzeichnis der im Garten des Erzherzoglichen Schlosses Weilburg benfindlichen Rosen"). 1834. Trans. by Eric Unmuth. Two photocopies.

Liste de 500 Variétés de premier choix. Comp. by J. Gravereaux. La Roseraie de l'Haÿ (Seine): 1900. Photocopy.

Macoboy, Stirling. *The Ultimate Rose Book.* New York: Harry Abrams, 1993.

Nottle, Trevor. *Growing Old-Fashioned Roses in Australia and New Zealand.* Kenthurst: Kangaroo Press, 1983.

Ovid. *Fasti.* Loeb Classical Library. 1931.

Parsons, Samuel B. *Parsons on the Rose.* New York: Orange Judd Company, 1888. Reprint. Stanfordville, N.Y.: Earl M. Coleman, 1979.

Paul, William. *The Rose Garden or The Rose Fancier's Manual.* London: Sherwood, Gilbert & Piper, 1848. Reprint. New York: Earl M. Coleman, 1978.

Phillips, Roger, and Martyn Rix. *Roses.* New York: Random House, 1988.

———. *The Quest for the Rose.* London: BBC Books; New York: Random House, 1993.

Pliny. *Natural History.* Loeb Classical Library. 1956.

Prince, William Robert. *Prince's Manual of Roses.* New York, 1846. Reprint. Stanfordville, N.Y.: Earl M. Coleman, 1979.

Pronville, Auguste de. *Nomenclature Raisonnée des Espèces, Variétés et Sous-Variétés du Genre Rosier . . . des environs de Paris.* Paris: De l'Imprimerie et dans la Librairie de Madame Huzard (née Vallat la Chapelle), 1818.

Rivers, Thomas. *The Rose Amateur's Guide.* London: Longman, Brown, Green & Longman, 1846. Reprint. Stanfordville, N.Y.: Earl M. Coleman, 1979.

Shepherd, Roy E. *History of the Rose.* New York: Macmillan Co., 1954. Reprint. New York: Earl M. Coleman, 1978.

Simon, Léon, and Pierre Cochet. *Nomenclature de tous les Noms des Roses connus . . . couleur et synonymes.* 2d ed. Paris: Librairie Horticole, 1906.

Steen, Nancy. *The Charm of Old Roses.* Washington, D.C.: Milldale Press, 1987.

Thomas, Graham Stuart. *The Old Shrub Roses.* rev. ed. London: J. M. Dent & Sons, 1983.

———. *Shrub Roses of Today.* rev. ed. London: J. M. Dent & Sons, 1985.

———. ed. *A Garden of Roses: Watercolors by Alfred Parsons.* Topsfield, Mass.: Salem House Publishers, 1987.

———. *Gardening with Roses.* New York: Henry Holt & Co., 1991.

———. *The Graham Stuart Thomas Rose Book.* Portland, Oreg.: Sagapress/Timber Press, 1994.

Werger, Joanne, and Robert E. Burton. *Roses: A Bibliography of Botanical, Horticultural, and Other Works Related to the Genus Rosa.* Metuchen, N.J.: Scarecrow Press, 1972.

In addition to the above and the current catalogs from the nurseries listed under "Rose Specialists," the rose inventory lists of Roseraie de l'Haÿ (1992), Rosarium Sangerhausen 1988), and Park Wilhelmshöhne (1987) have been consulted.

Sources & Resources

Mail-order Rose Specialists

[Catalog/price-list costs vary and change. Please inquire. If inquiring by mail, enclose a self-addressed stamped envelope. For inquiries by mail to nurseries outside the US, enclose an international reply coupon, available through the postal service.]

Australia

Reliable Roses
George Road
Silvan, Victoria, 3795 Australia
Telephone: (Country code: 61) 03
  9737-9313

The Rose Garden
(Walter Duncan Roses)
P.O. Box 18
Watervale, SA 5172
Australia

Belgium

Pépinières Louis Lens S.A.
Redinnestraat 11
8460 Oudenburg, Belgium
Telephone: (Country code: 32) 059-
  26 78 30
Fax: (Country code: 32) 059-26 56
  14

Denmark

Rosenplanteskolen i Løve
Plantevej 3, 4270 Høng
Denmark
Telephone: (Country code: 45) 45 53
  56 93 13
Fax: (Country code: 45) 53 59 90 19

Canada

Carl Pallek & Son Nurseries
Box 137, Virgil
Ontario L0S 1T0 Canada
Telephone: (905) 468-7262
Canadian orders only.

Hardy Roses for the North
Box 2048, Grand Forks
British Columbia V0H 1H0 Canada
Telephone: (604) 442-8442
Fax: (604) 442-2766

Hortico
723 Robson Road, RR 1, Waterdown
Ontario L0K 2H1 Canada Telephone:
  (905) 689-6984
Fax: (905) 689-6566

Pickering Nurseries, Inc.
670 Kingston Road, Pickering
Ontario L1V 1A6 Canada
Telephone: (905) 839 2111
Fax: (905) 839-4807

England

David Austin Roses
Bowling Green Lane
Albrighton, Wolverhampton
WV7 3HB England
Telephone: (Country code: 44) 01902
  373931
Fax: (Country code: 44) 01902 372
  142

Peter Beales Roses
London Road, Attleborough
Norfolk, NR17 1AX
England
Telephone: (Country code: 44) 01953
  454707
Fax: (Country code: 44) 01953
  456845

France

Les Roses Anciennes de André Eve
B.P. 206
28, Morailles, Pithiviers-le-Viel
45302, Pithiviers, France
Telephone: (Country Code: 33) 16 38
  30 01 30
Fax: (Country Code: 33) 16 38 30 71
  65

Roseraie de Berty
07110 Largentiere
France
Telephone: (Country Code: 33) 75 88
  30 56
Fax: (Country Code: 33) 75 88 36 93

Germany

Ingwer J. Jensen GmbH
Am Schloßprak 2b
24960 Glücksburg, Germany
Telephone: (Country code: 49) 04631
  60100
Fax: (Country Code: 49) 04631 2080

Rosen von Schultheis
Bad Nauheimer Str. 3-7
612 31 Bad Nauheim-Steinfurth
Germany
Telephone: (Country code: 49) 06032
  81013
Fax: (Country code: 49) 06032 85890

Italy

Rose and Rose Emporium
Contrada Fossalto 9
05015 Fabro (Terni) Italy
Telephone: (Country Code: 39) 0763
  82812
Fax: (Country Code: 39) 0763 82828

New Zealand

Trevor Griffiths Roses
No. 3, R.D., Timaru
New Zealand
Telephone: (Country code: 64) 03
  615-7722
Fax. (Country Code: 64) 03-615-7722

United States

The Antique Rose Emporium
Route 5 Box 143
Brenham, TX 77833
Telephone: (409) 836-9051
Fax: (409) 836-0928

Blossoms and Bloomers
East 11415 Krueger Lane
Spokane, WA 99207
Telephone (509) 922-1344

Hardy Roses for the North
P.O. Box 273
Danville WA 99121-0273
Telephone: (604) 442-8442
Fax: (604) 442-2766

Heritage Rosarium
211 Haviland Mill Road
Brookeville, MD 20833
Telephone: (301) 774-2806

Heritage Rose Gardens
16831 Mitchell Creek Drive
Fort Bragg, CA 95437
Telephone: (707) 964-3748

Heirloom Old Garden Roses
24062 NE Riverside Drive RG
St. Paul, OR 97137
Telephone: (503) 538-1576
Fax: (503) 538-5902

Lowe's Own-Root Roses
6 Sheffield Road
Nashua, NH 03062-3028
Telephone: (603) 888-2214

The Roseraie at Bayfields
P.O. Box R
Waldoboro, ME 04572-0919
Telephone: (207) 832-6330
Fax: Same as above

Spring Valley Roses
N7637 330th Street
Spring Valley, WI 54767
Telephone (715) 778-4481

Vintage Gardens
2227 Gravenstein Highway South
Sebastopol, CA 95472
Telephone: (707) 829-2035

To obtain permit to import roses:

Permit Unit
United States Department of Agriculture
Plant Protection and Quarantine Programs
Federal Building, Room 632
6505 Belcrest Road
Hyattsville, MD 20782

Societies

American Rose Society
Membership Secretary
P.O. Box 30,000
Shreveport, LA 71130
(318) 938-5407

Bermuda Rose Society
Box PG162
Paget 6, Bermuda

Canadian Rose Society
Anne Graber
10 Fairfax Crescent
Scarborough, Ontario
M1L 1Z8 Canada

Dallas Area Historical Society
P.O. Box 38585
Dallas, TX 75238-0585

Heritage Rose Group
c/o Mrs. Bev Dodson
1034 Taylor Avenue
Alameda CA 94501

Heritage Roses Australia
56 Gilford Street
Kariong, NSW 2572, Australia

Heritage Roses New Zealand
"Lyddington," R.D. 1
Rangiora, New Zealand

Roses Anciennes en France
Mme. Francoise Kauss,
5 Chemin des Balmes
F69110 Ste. Foy Les Lyon, France

Royal National Rose Society
Historical Roses Group
Lt. Col. Kenneth J. Grapes,
Chiswell Green, St. Albans
Hertfordshire, AL2 3NR England

Verein Deutscher Rosenfreunde
Geschaefsstelle-VDR, Waldseestrasse
  14
D-76530 Baden-Baden, Germany

Note: Issued annually, the *Combined Rose List* is available from Peter Schneider, P.O. Box 677, Mantua OH 44255.

Gardens

Göteborg Rosarium
c/o Gotenborgs Fritidsforvaltnig
Slottskogen-Tradgardsforeningen
Box 225
401-23 Göteborg Sweden

Huntington Botanical Gardens
1151 Oxford Road
San Marino CA 91108 USA

Mottisfont Abbey Garden
Mottisfont, near Romsey
Hampshire, SO51 0LJ England

Rosarium Sangerhausen
Steinberger Weg
4700 Sangerhausen Germany

Roseraie de l'Haÿ
Rue Albert Watel
94240 L'Haÿ des Roses, France

Schloss Wilhelmshöhe
Gartenverwaltung
34125 Kassel, Hessen, Germany

Index

[See page 21 for explanation of boldface type, alphabetization, and cross references.]

African Black. See 'Africaine'.

A Fruit en Poire ('Pear-Fruited Rose'). Prévost, France, 1826. Large, semi-double, rich clear pink marbled with paler pink. Vigorous, spreading growth.

Agamide ('Agamede'). Vibert, France, 1836. Mid-sized, full, reflexed flowers of rich rose color, spotted with white. Daughter of King Augeas whose stables were cleaned by Hercules.

Agar [#1]   **25**

Agar [#2]. Laffay, France. Deep cerise flowers.

Agates Desfosses. Before 1848. Mid-size, double, pale blush blossoms.

Agatha   **25**

Agathe roses   **25**

Agathe Abondante. Purple.

Agathe à Dix Coeurs. Lahaye, France, before 1836. Small, full, light lilac-pink blooms with paler edges.

Agathe Admirable. Miellez, France. Rose-pink. Date of 1860 appears in texts; however, this would be after the heyday of Gallicas.

Agathe à Feuilles Glauques. E. Noisette, France, before 1836. Full, delicate pink blooms in clusters.

Agathe Agréable. Miellez, France, 1860(?). Pink.

Agathe à la Mode. Crimson.

Agathe Alba. Before 1845. White.

Agathe Amédé. Desportes, France, 1827. Pink.

Agathe Amusante. Miellez, France, 1860(?). Pink.

Agathe Anaïs. Noisette, France, 1827. Pink.

Agathe Anémone Argent. Purple, shaded violet.

Agathe Angelina. Vibert, France, 1824.

Agathe Anna. Vétillard, France, before 1840. Bright rose-pink.

Agathe Antilope. Vibert, France. Purple.

Agathe Antonia. Vibert, France, 1823.

Agathe à Petites Fleurs. Before 1834.

Agathe Athala. Garilland, France, before 1840. Pink.

Agathe Aurelie. Before 1845. Bright pink.

Agathe Belle Carnée. Pelletier, France, before 1836. Pink and purple.

Agathe Bien Aimée. Before 1834.

Agathe Boursault ('Mme Boursault'). Noisette, France, 1827. White, shaded pink.

Agathe Brigitte. Vibert, France, 1821. Purple-violet.

Agathe Carnée. Before 1813. White blushed pink. In Joséphine's collection at Malmaison.

Agathe Cécile. Leroy. 1825.

Agathe Clarisse. Hardy, France, 1824. Pale pink.

Agathe Crépue du Roi [#1]. Pink color.

Agathe Crépue du Roi [#2]. White.

Agathe de Bruxelles. Pink.

Agathe de Constantine. Deep pink.

Agathe de Corne. Clear pink.

Agathe de Couleur de Soie. Miellez, France, 1836. Rose color.

Agathe de la Malmaison. Pelletier, France, before 1813. Double pale pink blooms. In Joséphine's collection.

Agathe de Montmorency. Blush white.

Agathe de Provence. Silvery pink.

Agathe de Rome. Belgium, 1825. Medium, very full, blush pink.

Agathe du Brésil. Flesh pink.

Agathe Élégante. Hardy, France, 1823. Blush pink.

Agathe en Plumet. Miellez, France, before 1836. Large, double, vivid pink.

Agathe Fatima. See 'Agathe Fatime'.

Agathe Fatime   26

Agathe Favorite ('Agathe Prolifère'). Prévost, France, before 1834. Small, double, bright flesh pink.

Agathe Félicite Boîtard. Pale pink.

Agathe Gentilhomme. Gentilhomme. Pink.

Agathe Grande. Before 1834. Flesh pink.

Agathe Grande Nouvelle. Descemet, France, before 1820. Flesh pink and purple.

Agathe Hybrida Revoluta. Descemet.

Agathe Hyon. Lilac-pink.

Agathe Incarnata   26, **27**

Agathe Incomparable ('Agathe Invincible'). Prévost, France, before 1836. Small, very double, rich purple-pink.

Agathe Invincible. See 'Agathe Incomparable'.

Agathe Magnifique. Holland, before 1834. Bright pink.

Agathe Majestueuse ('Boule d'Hortensia'). Godefroy, France, before 1830. Clear pink.

Agathe Marie Louise. See 'Duchesse d'Angoulême' [#1].

Agathe Nankin Derlin. Salmon pink.

Agathe Nouvelle ('Nouvelle Héloise', 'Elouise') Descemet, France, before 1814. Medium, full pale pink, shaded purple-crimson.

Agathe Ombrée ('Lady Jeanne Grey', 'Jeanne Grey'). Lahaye, France, before 1838. Medium, very double, violet-pink blossoms, edged deep purple.

Agathe Parfaite ('Descemet', 'Didon', 'Parfaite Agathe'). Prévost, France, 1834. Lilac-pink. This rose is also attributed to Vibert, 1838. Possibly dual introduction.

Agathe Porcelaine. Prévost, France, before 1836. Small, very double, evenly colored light pink with paler circumference.

Agathe Précieuse. See 'Duchesse d'Angoulême' [#1].

Agathe Prolifère. See 'Agathe Favorite'.

Agathe Pyramidale Agréable. See 'Grande Sultane' [#4].

Agathe Renoncule. See 'Provins Renoncule'.

Agathe Renoncule Constante. Pink.

Agathe Royale   26

Agathe sans Pareille. Before 1834.

Agénor. Vibert, France, 1832; 1835 by Robert. Mid-size, double, reddish purple blooms. Phoenican king of Troy.

Aglaée Adanson. Vibert, France, 1823. Purple blossoms, shaded rose.

Aglaée de Marsilly. Vibert, France, 1818. Mid-size, very double, convex blossoms of pale pink.

Aglaia. Before 1813. In Joséphine's collection at Malmaison. Lilac-pink with white. One of the three Graces in Greek mythology. See below for the other two, Thalia and Euphrosine.

Agmète. Spotted pink.

Agnès Sorel ('Agnès Sorrel'). Vibert, France, 1820. Gallica-Centifolia hybrid. Very large, full, lilac-pink with an almost white circumference. Mistress of Charles VII.

Agnodice. Vibert, France, 1820. Very large, double, compact blossoms of lilac-rose. Branching growth.

A Grandes Corymbes. Joly, France, 1835. Violet-pink flowers.

A Grandes Feuilles. Lelieur, France. Deep pink blossoms with large foliage.

Agremont. Before 1846. Rose-carmine flowers with a white border.

Ahasuerus. Before 1848. Gallica-China hybrid. Bright crimson marbled with violet-crimson. In the Old Testament, ruler of the Persians.

Aigle Bleu. Violet purple with blue tones.

Aigle Brun. Godefroy, France, 1820. Mid-size, double, velvety purple blossoms. 'Aigle Brun' appears on Gravereaux's list of roses at Malmaison, yet other sources attribute the rose to Godefroy, 1820. Three possibilities follow: [#1] is lost, this is [#2]; or Godefroy could have claimed the Malmaison rose; or Joséphine's son Eugene could have added it since he was at Malmaison until 1824.

Aigle Brun Maculé ('Grand Maculée'). Coquerel, France. Large, semi-double, purple, spotted.

Aigle de Prusse. See 'La Veuve' [#2].

Aigle du Sérail. Purple blossoms.

Aigle Noir. Godefroy, France, 1818. Velvety purple.

Aimable Amie   26

Aimable Beauté. van Eeden, Holland, before 1834. Very double.

Aimable Emma. Pink blossoms with a paler border.

Aimable Fanny. Bright pink.

Aimable Henriette. Vibert, France, 1842. Mid-size, double, rose-crimson blossoms. Spotted.

Aimable Hortense. Vibert, France, before 1838. Profuse mid-size, full flowers of clear pink.

Aimable Lieutot. Pink.

Aimable Pourpre. Before 1813. In Joséphine's collection at Malmaison. Blackish purple.

Aimable Queen. Before 1848. Mid-sized, doubled, expanded flowers. Crimson aging to crimson-purple. Upright, vigorous growth.

Aimable Rose. 1819.

Aimable Rouge   29

Aimable Sophie ('Archduke Charles', 'Clemence Isaure'). Before 1834. Semi-double to double, soft pink blossoms with almost white circumference.

Aimable Tastu. Before 1848. Very double, purple flowers.

Aimable Violette.

Aimable Virginie. Deep pink.

Aimée. Vibert, France, 1823. Crimson, shaded darker.

Aimée Roman. Prévost, France, before 1838. Mid-size, very double, clear crimson-purple blossoms.

Ajax. Before 1834. Homeric hero.

Alain Blanchard   14, **28**, 29

Alain Blanchard Panachée. See 'Alain Blanchard'.

Alaine   29

Alba Regia Aureata. Small pink blossoms.

Alba Subviridis. Pale pink.

Albertine. Prévost, France, 1827. Mid-size, double, compact flowers of rose color, shaded purple and paling to lilac blush. Small, lax growth.

Alcibiade. Deep pink. Athenian general.

Alcime. Vibert, France, 1845. Mid-size, full flowers. Deep dark violet.

Alcine. Moreau-Robert, France, before 1848. Large, full, cupped and spotted rose-pink blooms with pale lilac circumference. Vigorous erect growth.

Aldebaran. Before 1848. Large, very double, cupped crimson flowers.

Aldégonde [#1] ('Grand Conde', 'Violette Brillanté', 'Rouge Formidable'). Godefroy, 1817. Medium, full. Purple violet.

Aldégonde [#2] ('Grand Clovis', 'Porcia', 'Pourpre Cramoisi'). Vibert, France, before 1820. Medium, full, strong lilac-pink to purple. Nearly thornless.

Alector Cramoisi. Before 1813. In Joséphine's collection at Malmaison. Velvety crimson.

Alette. 1845. Gallica-Centifolia hybrid. Large, double, globular, wax-like blush pink blooms.

Alexander Laquemont. See 'Alexandre Laquement'.

Alexandre Chatry. Purple-crimson blooms.

Alexandre Laquement   28, 29

Alexandrine. Velvety crimson.

Alfieri   29

Alice Vena   29

Alicia. Before 1848. Reddish lilac blossoms.

Alika   9, 31

Alix Diadème de Flore. See 'Diadème de Flore-Alix'.

Alphonse de Coster. Purple-pink.

Alphonse de Lamartine. Clear pink. Poet and politician.

Alphonse Maille. Boutigny, France, 1825. Gallica-China hybrid. Large double blooms, bright crimson, tinged purple and spotted rose. Upright vigorous growth.

Althénor. Blackish violet flowers.

Alvarez. Before 1848. Mid-size, full, crimson-purple flowers.

Alzine. Before 1848. Mid-size, full, rich rose-colored blossoms. Gallica-China hybrid.

Amanda. Before 1848. Mid-size, full, compact blooms of light purple-rose. Thornless. Upright growth.

Amarante. Crimson-amaranthe.

Amaryllis. 1818.

Ambroise Paré   31

Amelia. Prévost, France, before 1834. Cerise.

Amélie de Mansfield   31

Amelia d'Orléans. Cartier, France, 1825. Agathe rose. Large, very double, well-formed pale blush blossoms.

Ami Derair. Crimson, shaded.

Aminta. Descemet, France, before 1834.

Amiral Coligny. Pale pink. Commemorates the expansionist Gaspard de Coligny.

Amiral de Rigny. Noisette, France, 1827. Mid-size, double, white, shaded violet blossoms. Dark green foliage and long flower stalks.

Amitié   31

Amoureuse. Hardy, France, before 1846. Pink.

Amphitrite. Vibert, France, before 1838. Large, full cherry-crimson flowers. In Greek mythology, one of the Nereids, goddess of the sea and wife of Poseidon.

Anacréon   **30**, 31

Anais. Vibert, France, 1819. Lilac pink.

Anaïs Ségales   **30**, 31

Anarelle. Before 1846. Large, very full, cupped, well-formed blooms. Purplish rose. Lilac outer petals.

Anatole. Noisette, France, 1827. An Agathe rose. Medium, very double, bright crimson blooms in clusters.

Ancelin. Before 1848. Gallica-China hybrid. Medium, double, cupped blossoms of vivid rose-pink.

Ancien Diadème de Flore. See 'Diadème de Flore-Ancien'.

Andalusian. Before 1834.

Andersonii   31

André. Crimson and carmine.

André Dupont ('Pointiana'). Before 1813. In Joséphine's collection at Malmaison. Bright crimson. Foremost rosarian of his time.

André Fouquier. Deep crimson blossoms.

André Thouin ('Thouin'). Prévost, France, before 1834.

Mid-size, double, blossoms of vivid crimson, marbled purple.

Andromaque [#1] ('L'Amoureuse'). Vibert, France, 1816. Large double bright crimson blooms. Wife of Hector; heroine of the Racine tragedy.

Andromaque [#2]. Hardy, France. Deep pink.

Anémone Ancienne. See 'Ornement de la Nature'.

Anémone de Luxembourg. Hardy, France. Deep pink.

Angelique. Descemet, France. Deep crimson.

Angiola. Vibert, France, 1846. Gallica-Centifolia hybrid. Medium-size, double, white blossoms.

Anglica Major. Before 1834. Crimson.

Anna Kzartoryska ('Anna Czartoryski'). Vibert, France, 1845. Large, full, cupped blossoms of purplish crimson, mottled pink.

Anna Von Baden. Pink touched with green.

Anne de Boleyn. Girardon, France, before 1838. Large, double, blossom of blush pink with a green button eye. Compact growth to 2 feet. Second wife of Henry VIII (1507-1536).

Antenor. Deep rose flowers.

Antigone. Vibert, France, 1838. Medium, full, flesh pink blossoms. Heroine of Sophocles; daughter of Oedipus.

Antione. Crimson marbled blossoms.

Antiope. Descemet, France. Mid-size, very double, spotted, purplish-crimson flowers. Queen of the Amazons; sister of Hippolyta.

Antoine d'Ormois. See 'Antonia d' Ormois'.

Antonia. Before 1834. Variegated or striped blossoms.

Antonia d'Ormois   32, **33**

Antonica. Before 1848. Gallica-China hybrid. Medium, double, compact blooms. Blush with deeper rose center.

Antwerp. Before 1834.

A'Odeur d'Anisette. Vibert, France. 1842. Gallica-China hybrid. Medium, full, rose-colored blooms.

A'Odeur de Pâte d'Amande. Before 1848. Gallica-China hybrid. Medium, full, cupped crimson-rose blooms.

A Pétals Frangées. See 'Fimbriata à Pétals Frangées'.

Aphrodite. Noisette, France, before 1838. Clusters of flowers with slightly fringed petals. Violet, tinged with crimson. Compact shrub.

Apollon ('Superbe Cramoisie'). Robert, France, before 1848. Large, semi-double, cupped blooms. Crimson, shaded purple. Upright growth.

Apothecary's Rose. See 'Officinalis'.

A Rameux Sarmenteux. Robert, France, 1845. Mid-size, semi-double blossoms. Rose-pink striped violet.

Aramis   32

Archbishop of Mechlin. Belgium, 1825. Large, very full, rich pink blossoms, veined with crimson.

Archduke Charles. See 'Aimable Sophie'.

Archduke Luis. Before 1834.

Archevêque de Besançon. Before 1848. Gallica-China hybrid. Large, double, compact flowers. Rich rose tinted purple.

Archevêque de Cambray. Before 1834.

Archevêque de Malines. Belgium, 1825. Deep pink, veined crimson.

Archidamie. Hardy, France, 1825. Large, very full, well-formed flowers. Bright crimson.

Archiduchesse Dorothée. Germany. Crimson.

Ardoisée. France, before 1846. Large, double, deep rosy mauve.

Aréthuse (Perhaps also 'Arethusa'). Vibert, France, 1819. Small, double, bright purple blooms spotted with pink. Variegated leaves. From Greek myth, nymph turned into a fountain.

Argentine. Vibert, France, 1823.

Argus. Pink. One-hundred-eyed creature of Greek myth.

Ariadne   32

Aricie. Vibert, France, before 1838. Large to medium, deep pink blossoms with a mauve circumference. Shrine of Diana; or minor goddess.

Ariel. Before 1848. Very large, full rose-pink.

Aristide. Garilland, France, 1823. Violet. Athenian statesman.

Arlequin   32

Armande. Lahaye, France. Purple-violet.

Arsinoé. 1816.

Artèmise. Before 1846. Mid-size, double, compact reflexed blossoms. Rich dark purple streaked crimson. Centers rose-crimson. Upright growth.

Arthemise. 1819. Medium, full blossoms. Light vivid pink.

Arvina. Deep pink.

Asmodée. Vibert, France, 1849. Large, double, clear crimson blooms.

Aspasie [#1]. Vibert, France, 1819. Violet-purple. Consort of Pericles.

Aspasie [#2]. Vibert, France, before 1846. Gallica-Centifolia hybrid. Medium, full, cupped blossoms of flesh pink, aging to blush. Well-formed. Profuse bloom. Upright growth.

Assemblage de Beauté. See 'Assemblage des Beautés'.

Assemblage des Beautés   32, **33**

Astarade. Violet shaded.

Astéroïde. Before 1848. Gallica-China hybrid. Medium, very full blossoms of violet purple.

Atala [#1]. Vibert, France, 1845. Deep pink flowers.

Atala [#2]. Garilland, France. Light pink.

Atalante. Vibert, France, 1818. Pale pink flowers.

Athalie. Vibert, France, before 1838. Large, doubled, expanded blooms. Cherry crimson with some purple shading. Profuse bloom. Branching growth.

Athanais. Vibert, France, 1818. Clear pink blossoms.

Athelin. Crimson, spotted white.

Attala. 1845. Gallica-Centifolia hybrid. Large, double blossoms of blush white.

Aubert. Parmentier, Belgium. Pink and crimson flowers.

Augustine. Godefroy, France. Pale pink.

Augustine Bertin. Vibert, France, 1818. Pale pink blooms.

Augustine Pourprée. Pelletier, France, before 1838. Large, semi-double, velvety dark violet-purple blooms.

Augustine Sans Épines. Godefroy, France. Same as above but without thorns.

Aurelia. Before 1834.

Aurélie Delamarre. V. Verdier, France, 1847. Pink blossoms, shaded.

Aurélie Lemaire. Before 1848. Medium, double, globular rose-colored blossoms. Well-formed. Shiny foliage. Upright growth.

Aurélie Lemarc. Before 1846. Well-formed, vivid rose-pink blooms spotted with white.

Aurora. Before 1846. Gallica-China hybrid. Large, full-cupped blossoms of bright rose sometimes shaded with violet. The petals often have a white streak in the center. Greek goddess of the dawn.

Aurore. See 'Helvetia'.

Aurore d'Enghein. Parmentier, Belgium. Deep rose.

Aurore Helvetia. See 'Helvetia'.

Austrica ('Austrian'). Cerise.

Autumn Damask. See 'Quatre Saisons'.

Auzou ('Couture'). Cartier, France, before 1846. Gallica-China hybrid. Medium, full, compact, carmine flowers, marbled with purple. Occasionally with a crimson center.

Avenant   34

Avocat Laloup. Before 1848. Medium, double, globular blooms of bright cherry-rose, aging to violet.

Axmannii. Flesh-pink.

Azélie ('Azelia Rose'). Miellez, France, before 1838. Gallica-Centifolia hybrid. Small to mid-size, double, pale flesh-colored blossoms.

Azéma. Vibert, France, before 1838. Mid-size, double, pale blush.

Bacchante   34

Bachelier. Deep flesh pink blossoms.

Bacou. Pale pink.

Balbise. Noisette, France, 1827. Pink spotted white.

Bambolina. Noisette, France, 1823. Purple flowers.

Bance. Pink blossoms, marbled.

Bandeau de Soliman ('Charles X', 'La Napolitaine', 'L'Esponia', 'Raucourt', 'Ulysse' 'Lesponda'). Prévost, France. Velvety purple-crimson.

Bandeau Nuptial. Before 1838. Medium, very double, cupped blush blossoms with a rose center.

Banestu ('Baneste Pourpre'). Calvert, France, before 1838. Medium, double, rich crimson-purple blossoms.

Baragay ('Baraguey'). Hardy, France. Ashen pink.

Barbanigra. See 'Temple d'Apollon'.

Barbe à Négre. See 'Temple d'Apollon'.

Barbinegra. See 'Temple d'Apollon'.

Baron Cuvier. Before 1848. Large, doubled, cupped, dark rose, paling to violet with age. Upright growth.

Baron de Gossard   34

Baron de Staël. See 'Baronne de Staël'.

Baron de Warez. Deep purple.

Baron Louis ('Le Baron Louis'). Vibert, France, before 1848. Medium, double, purple. Spotted white. Cerise-rose center. Upright growth.

Baronne de Saint-Cyr. Guerin, France.

Baronne de Staël ('Baron de Staël'). Vibert, France, 1820. Large, full, deep bright pink blossoms with darker veining. Vigorous branching growth. Madame de Staël, famous author (1766-1817), so named in her honor?

Baronne d'Ivry. Deep crimson.

Batarde de Roi. Before 1838. A hybrid, of course. Gallica-Centifolia. Large, double, nodding, bright pink blooms. (With such a name, it is a shame this is lost!)

Baucis. 1820. Medium, double, cupped rose-crimson blooms, well spotted with violet. Branching growth. From Ovid, a humble peasant transformed into an oak.

Bazaris. Before 1838. Small, full, soft pink with an almost white circumference. Few thorns.

Beau Narcisse   34

Beauregard. Miellez, France. Dark purple.

Beauté Brillanté. Miellez, France. Deep crimson.

Beauté Choisie. Holland. Crimson blossoms.

Beauté Cramoisie. France, 1816. Crimson.

Beauté Criante. Before 1834.

Beauté de la Malmaison   34

Beauté du Jour. Miellez, France, before 1838. Gallica-Centifolia hybrid(?). Medium to large, bright deep rose-color blooms; outer petals pale to soft lilac.

Beauté Fine. Miellez, France. Pink blossoms.

Beauté Flatteuse. Miellez, France. Crimson.

Beauté Frappante. Holland, before 1834. Purple-violet.

Beauté Incomparable. Miellez, France. Crimson.

Beauté Insurmontable. Holland, before 1834. Crimson.

Beauté of Billiard ('Docteur Billiard'). Gallica-China hybrid. Medium, double, bright scarlet-crimson. Later blooming than most other Gallicas.

Beauté Pâle. Miellez, France. Flesh pink.

Beauté Parfaite ('Unique Admirable'). Holland, before 1848. Double, bright violet-crimson. See note under 'Unique Admirable'.

Beauté Pourpre. Before 1834. Medium, double, bright clear purple.

Beauté Rare. Miellez, France. Bright vivid crimson.

Beauté Riante. Miellez, France, before 1834. Small, very full, convex, rich deep pink with paler edges.

Beauté Rouge. Before 1834. Crimson.

Beauté Sans Pareille. Before 1834.

Beauté Sauvage. Before 1848. Very large, double, compact, vivid rose-pink.

Beauté Superbe. Before 1813. In Joséphine's collection at Malmaison. Clear crimson blooms.

Beauté Surprenante. Descemet, France, before 1813. Medium, full, blush pink, almost white. Nearly thornless. In Joséphine's collection at Malmaison.

Beauté Tendre. Dupont, France.

Beauté Tendre Cramoisie. Before 1838. Large, very double, well-formed blooms. Bright crimson.

Beauté Touchante. Miellez, France, before 1813. In Joséphine's collection at Malmaison. Crimson.

Beauté Triomphante. Before 1834.

Beauté Vive. Before 1848. Gallica-China hybrid. Medium, full, compact, light but bright crimson. Small branching growth.

Beauvelours. See 'Passe Velours'.

Beethoven. Before 1848. Double, cupped, rose-pink.

Belgica Rubra ('Vitex Spinosa'). Godefroy, France, 1817. Large, semi-double bright crimson. Dark green leaves.

Bella Doria. See 'Belle Doria'.

Bellard   34

Bellart. See 'Bellard'.

Bella Victoria. Velvety crimson flowers.

Belle Abellina. Miellez, France. Flesh pink.

Belle Actrice. Holland, before 1834. Purple.

Belle Adélaïde. Miellez, France. Very full, flattened, cerise.

Belle Africaine. See 'Africaine'.

Belle Agathe. Pink.

Belle Aimable. Before 1813. Light crimson, spotted white. In Joséphine's collection at Malmaison.

Belle Alice. Parmentier, Belgium. Blush pink.

Belle Alliance. See 'Tricolore' [#1].

Belle Alzindor. Before 1848. Medium, double, compact vivid rose-pink, aging to mauve. Branching growth.

Belle Amante. Holland. Crimson.

Belle Amazone. Miellez, France. Crimson.

Belle Armide. Before 1834.

Belle Arsène. Miellez, France. Crimson flowers.

Belle Aspasie. Before 1838. Very large, semi-double, bright velvety purple.

Belle Astelle. Vibert, France.

Belle Auguste [#1] ('Empereur Auguste'). Vibert, France, 1817. White and flesh pink.

Belle Auguste [#2]. Before 1838. Deep purple.

Belle Aurore. See 'Lee' [#1].

Belle Biblis   34

Belle Bigottini. Laffay, France, 1825. Lilac blooms.

Belle Bourbon. Violet-purple.

Belle Brune [#1]. Before 1813. In Joséphine's collection at Malmaison. Purple-violet blooms.

Belle Brune [#2]. Lartay, France, 1861. Crimson.

Belle Camellia. France. Shades of purple.

Belle Catalani. 1826. Large pink blooms with paler blush circumference.

Belle Cerise. Descemet, France, before 1834. Crimson.

Belle Charlotte. Purple.

Belle Charmante. Before 1834.

Belle Charmante Pourpre. Before 1834.

Belle Chartonnaise. Violet-purple flowers.

Belle Courtesan. Before 1848. Gallica-China hybrid. Medium, double, flesh pink blooms with blush outer petals.

Belle Cramoisie. Robert, France, before 1834. Medium, double, globular blossoms. Purple, mauve, and bright crimson blend. Vigorous upright growth.

Belle Cramoisie Formosa. Calvert, France. Crimson.

Belle d'Antonie. Before 1834.

Belle d'Aunay ('Belle d'Aulnay'). Prévost, France, before 1834. Very large, semi-double, clear soft pink.

Belle de Cels ('Grande Couronnée', 'Porcelaine', 'Pallidor', 'Damascena Mutabilis', 'Grande Renommée', 'La Coquette', 'La Pyramidale', 'Varin'). Descemet, France, before 1834. Gallica-Centifolia hybrid. Large, semi-double, pale clear blush pink paling to white. Considering the mess of names surrounding this rose, someone in history must have chuckled when naming it 'Grand Renommée'. *Renommer* as a verb is "to name again," as an adjective, "celebrated."

Belle de Charonne. Before 1848. Medium, double, violet-purple.

Belle de Crécy   15, 34, **35**

Belle de Damas. Pale pink blossoms.

Belle de Desbrosses ('Desbrosses'). Before 1838. Medium, full, compact, well-formed, rose-pink with a pale lilac circumference, in clusters. Vigorous upright growth.

Belle de Falmouth. Before 1834.

Belle de Fleury. Before 1834.

Belle de Fontenay. Boutigny, France, before 1838. Medium, full, white-edged vivid cherry-pink to pink-edged crimson. Small branching growth.

Belle de Hesse. See 'La Glorieuse' [#1].

Belle de Jour Pâle Riche en Fleurs ('Riche en Fleurs'). Before 1834.

Belle de Marly. Before 1848. Large, double, vivid rose-pink, shaded violet.

Belle de Parabere. Before 1848. Gallica-China hybrid. Large, full, globular, rose-lilac.

Belle de Parny. See 'La Tenterelle'.

Belle des Jardins   36

Belle de Stors. Lahaye, France. Clear purple.

Belle de Trianon. Prévost, France, before 1838. Medium, very full, pale flesh pink, aging almost white.

Belle de Vaucresson. Prévost, France, before 1848. Gallica-Centifolia hybrid. Medium, very double, flesh pink blooms.

Belle de Vernier. Before 1848. Gallica-China hybrid. Medium, full, cupped rose-crimson, mottled purple-gray.

Belle Devise. Flesh pink blooms, shaded.

Belle de Yèbles   36

Belle de Zelbes. Before 1848. Blush with rose circumference.

Belle Diane. Miellez, France. Purple.

Belle Didon. Pink with a crimson center.

Belle d'Ivrée. See 'Belle d'Yvry'.

Belle Doria   36

Belle Dorothée. Deep carmine.

Belle Douasienne. Miellez, France, before 1848. Medium, full, compact, pale lilac and pink.

Belle d'Yvry ('Belle d'Ivrée'). Before 1848. Gallica-China hybrid. Large, full, rose-lilac bloom shaded purple.

Belle Écossaise. Wine and violet blossoms.

Belle Elèonore ('Princesse Elèonore'). Miellez, France, 1824. A Gallica-Centifolia hybrid. Large, full, clear crimson.

Belle Elodie. Pink spotted violet.

Belle Émilie. Miellez, France, before 1838. Medium, very full, deep pink with fine spots.

Belle Émilie d'Arlon. David, 1839. Pink and white.

Belle Esquermoise. Miellez, France, before 1834. Crimson, striped mauve.

Belle Esquimaux. Before 1834. Large, double, deep pink blossoms shaded crimson-purple.

Belle Ferroniere. Before 1848. Gallica-China hybrid. Very large, full, soft rose-color. Crimson center.

Belle Flore [#1]. Descemet, France.

Belle Flore [#2]. See 'Fornarina'.

Belle Florentine. Boutigny, France, before 1834. Large, full, soft pink. Very small buds. Thornless.

Belle Florine. Miellez, France. Crimson.

Belle Forme. Before 1834. Crimson blossoms.

Belle Galathée   36

Belle George. Before 1834.

Belle Gris de Lin. Miellez, France. Deep flesh pink.

Belle Havraise. Bright crimson flowers.

Belle Hébè. Laffay, France, before 1813. Pink with darker stripes. In Joséphine's collection.

Belle Hélène [#1]. Decemet, France. Pale pink.

Belle Hélène [#2]   36

Belle Héloise. Laffay, France, before 1848. Gallica-China hybrid. Large, double, lilac-pink veined rose.

Belle Herminie [#1]. Vibert, France, 1822. Large, double, deep rose-colored flowers.

Belle Herminie [#2]. Vibert, France, 1822. Large blossoms. Violet-purple and mottled.

Belle Herminie [#3]. Before 1846. Semi-double blooms. Wine-crimson, spotted vivid pink.

Belle Herminie [#4]. Vibert, France, 1823. Very large, semi-double blossoms of rich dark rose. Marbled.

Belle Herminie [#5]. Vibert, France, 1824. Large, semi-double. Bright pink, spotted white.

Belle Herminie [#6]   36, 37

Belle Herminie Double. Vibert, France, 1824. Mid-sized, cherry-pink flowers marbled crimson-rose.

Belle Hollandaise. Miellez, France. Pink.

Belle Hortense. Miellez, France, before 1838. Gallica-Centifolia hybrid. Very large, very full, pink blooms with darker centers.

Belle Hyacinthe. Miellez, France. Pink blossoms.

Belle Impératrice. Pink.

Belle Incarnata. Holland, before 1834. Flesh pink.

Belle Isis   37

Belle Jenny. Before 1834.

Belle Jules. Vétillard, France, 1826.

Belle Junon [#1] ('Junon'). Pink with darker spots.

Belle Junon [#2] ('Rouge Agréable'). Prévost, France, before 1813. Small, double, clear pink. Profuse bloom. In Joséphine's collection at Malmaison.

Belle Kallos. Blush white flowers.

Belle Lauré. Miellez, France. before 1834. Crimson.

Belle Leopoldine. Boutigny, France. Clear pink.

Belle Lilloise. Miellez, France, 1859. Vermillion.

Belle Lise. Carmine-pink.

Belle Louise. Pink, shaded.

Belle Lucille. Descemet, France.

Belle Magdeleine. Duranche, 1823.

Belle Marbrée. Flesh pink.

Belle Marguerite. Cream, spotted white.

Belle Marie. Before 1834. Gallica-China hybrid. Large, full, cupped, rose-pink with paler edges.

Belle Merveilleuse. Miellez. Flesh pink.

Belle Mignonne ('Petite Louise'). Prévost, France, before 1834. Small, full, blush pink, well-formed blossoms. Inner petals often striped with white.

Belle Mode. Miellez, France, before 1838. Medium, full, crimson-purple with violet circumference.

Belle Ninon. Boutigny, France, before 1838. Medium, double, dark lilac. Lighter circumference.

Belle Octavie. Pale pink, darker veins.

Belle Olymphe. Descemet, France, before 1813. In Joséphine's collection at Malmaison. Crimson.

Belle Panachée. Holland. Clear purple, spotted mauve.

Belle Parade   38

Belle Parure. Miellez, France. Pink.

Belle Portugaise. Before 1848. Gallica-Centifolia hybrid. Large, double, cupped, purple-lilac.

Belle Pourpre   38

Belle Pourpre Violet. Descemet, France. Violet-purple blossoms.

Belle Rosalie de La Croix. Crimson.

Belle Rosine   38

Belle Rouge. Before 1834. Crimson.

Belle sans Flatterie   38, 39

Belle sans Pareille. Before 1834.

Belle Satinée. Before 1848. Medium, full, compact, even rose-pink. Erect growth.

Belle Splendens. Descemet, France.

Belle Sylvain. Before 1846. White with blush center.

Belle Ternaux. Boutigny, France, before 1838. Medium, full, well-formed, violet-purple blossoms with darker shading.

Belle Théophile. Prévost, France, before 1838. Medium, full, flesh pink. Blooms in clusters.

Belle Thérèse. Violet-purple flowers.

Belle Thurette. Before 1848. Gallica-China hybrid. Small, double, expanded blooms. Crimson, shaded purple.

Belle Villageoise. Vibert, France, 1839. Violet, spotted white. See discussion under 'Village Maid'.

Belle Violette ('La Belle Violette'). Vibert, France, before 1834. An Agathe rose. Medium, double, deep violet flowers.

Belle Violette de Lille. Violet.

Belle Violette Foncé. Descemet, France. Violet.

Belle Virginie   38

Belle Vue. Before 1834.

Belle Zurette. Before 1834.

Bellone. Miellez, France. Cerise pink.

Benjamin Constant. Garilland, France. Pink. French author Henri Benjamin Constant de Rebecque (1767-1830).

Benjamin Mary. Crimson and violet blooms.

Bennfous. Before 1834.

Benyowski ('Beniowski'). Coquerel, France, before 1838. Medium, full, purple-crimson occasionally spotted pink on outer petals.

Béquet. Before 1848. Gallica-China hybrid. Medium, double, expanded blooms. Rich carmine marbled with crimson-purple.

Béranger   38

Bérenice   38

Berkshire. Before 1834.

Berlèze. Robert, France, before 1846. Medium, doubled, expanded blossoms of brownish violet, shaded with mauve and spotted. Vigorous upright growth.

Berminade. Before 1834.

Berryer. Flesh pink.

Bertha. Before 1848. Large, full, creamy white.

Berthet. Cartier, France. Violet blossoms.

Bicolor. Before 1844. Semi-double vivid crimson blooms with a white stripe on each petal.

Bijou d'Enghien ('Brillant d'Enghien'). Holland, before 1848. Large, double, compact, rose-pink.

Bijou des Amateurs   38

Bizarre. Calvert, France, before 1838. Small, full blooms. Deep pink to soft purple.

Bizarre Changeant. See 'Arlequin'.

Bizarre de la Chine. Laffay, France, before 1834. Gallica-China hybrid. Clear purple.

Bizarre Flammé. Possibly from Belgium, 1822. Medium, bright crimson, shaded soft violet.

Bizarre Marbré ('Cécile Boireau'). Before 1846. Large, very double, well-formed. Vivid rich rose-pink marbled with blush. Profuse bloom.

Bizarre Pintade. Toutain, France, 1823. Violet, spotted white.

Bizarre sans Fruit. Joly, France, 1835. Pink.

Bizarre Triomphant ('Rose Bleu', 'Slate-colored Rose'). Descemet, France, before 1813. Medium, double, blue-slate to purple, streaked with dark lilac. In Joséphine's collection at Malmaison. The English synonym, 'Slate-colored Rose', is from Gore, who frequently translated French rose names.

Black Ranunculus Rose of Holland. See 'La Reine des Roses'.

Blanche de Castille ('Blanche of Castille'). Vibert, France, 1822. Possibly a Gallica-Centifolia hybrid. Medium, full, delicate blush pink. Very thorny.

Blanche Fleur   40

Blanche Hocidé. Large, double, cupped, soft rose blooms spotted with white.

Blandine [#1]. Before 1834. White.

Blandine [#2]. Vibert, France, 1845. Gallica-Centifolia hybrid. Large, full, globular, white.

Blondel de Vienne. Parmentier, Belgium. Lilac-pink.

Blood. Dark Crimson. (What a name and in English! At best, a color sense is given.)

Bloomerick. Clear pink.

Blush Gallica 40

Blush Minon. Before 1834.

Boieldieu ('Boildieu'). Prévost, France, 1828. Large, double, compact, clear soft rose.

Bonheur du Jour. Bright crimson.

Bonne Genevieve. Laffay, France, before 1848. Gallica-China hybrid. Double, compact, rich purple with a crimson center.

Bonté. Before 1834. Striped blossoms.

Bossuet 41

Botzaris. Robert, France, 1836. Clear pink blossoms. Not the white Damask now in commerce.

Bouclier d'Astolphe [#1]. Lecomte, France, before 1838. Large, double, well-formed blooms. Bright deep crimson.

Bouclier d'Astolphe [#2]. Savroureux, France. Violet-crimson.

Bouflers. Vibert. France. Lilac.

Boule de Nanteuil 40, 41

Boule de Neige [#1] ('Globe Blanc'). Calvert, France, (1826?). Gallica-Centifolia hybrid. Semi-double, globular white.

Boule de Neige [#2] ('Globe White Hip'). Vibert, France.

Boule d'Hortensia. See 'Agathe Majesteuse'.

Boulette. Before 1834.

Bouquet Charmant 41

Bouquet Choisi. Before 1834.

Bouquet de Miellez. Miellez, France. Deep crimson.

Bouquet de Muhlenheck. Bauman, France.

Bouquet de Otto. Bauman, France.

Bouquet de Vénus 41

Bouquet Joli. Lerouge, France.

Bouquet Ornement. Before 1834.

Bouquet Panachée. Before 1834.

Bouquet Parfait. See 'Agathe Royale'.

Bouquet Pourpre ('Mine d'Or'). France, 1814. Medium, crimson, spotted very dark purple. Blooms in clusters.

Bouquet Rose. Before 1834.

Bouquet Superbe. See 'Bouquet Charmant'.

Bouquet Tendre. Lerouge, France.

Bouquet Triomphant. Miellez, France. Pink.

Bourbon Nigra. Deep purple.

Bourgeois Gentilhomme. Before 1848. Medium, full, expanded, bright cherry, spotted soft lilac. Ground color pales to lilac. Profuse bloom. Upright growth. Named after the comedy by Moliere.

Brabant de la Fontaine. Before 1848. Vivid cherry with shading.

Bracelet d'Amour. Calvert, France, before 1838. Medium, very double, convex, lilac-rose paling at circumference.

Brennus 41

Breon. A crimson Gallica-China Hybrid.

Bridget. Before 1838. Mid-size, double, rich velvety violet-purple with bright crimson center.

Brillant d'Enghien. See 'Bijou d'Enghien'.

Brillanté. Descemet, France. Pink.

Briseis. 1817. Medium, full, soft pink. There is some indication that two roses from this period were given this name; the other, a China. Woman who was subject of quarrel between Agamemnon and Achilles.

Britannicus ('Lady Tankerville', 'Lady Thenermill', 'Manteau Impérial', 'Pourpre Obscur', 'Velvet-violet Ranunculus'). Godefroy, France, 1821. Small, full, velvety, deep violet-purple blooms.

Brown's Superb. Before 1848. Very large and double, globular, rose-crimson with a blush circumference. Wm. Paul noted that this is sometimes classified as a Bourbon rose; but as it was in cultivation before the Bourbons were known, he considered 'Brown's Superb' to be an Odorata-Gallica hybrid.

Brune Magnifique. Crimson, shaded.

Brunette. Descemet, France, before 1834. Medium, doubled, expanded, vivid crimson marbled purple.

Brunette Aimable. van Eeden, Holland, before 1834.

Buffon. Before 1848. Large, double, violet-purple.

Buonaparte. Before 1848. Large, double, compact, hemispherical blooms. Purple-rosy pink. Upright growth.

Busard Triomphant. Velvety crimson blossoms. Triomphant Buzzard? Who named this rose? Great for planting next to 'Blood', no doubt.

Cadische. Pink.

Calife de Bagdad. Miellez, France. Lilac.

Calypso. Descemet, France, before 1813. Named by Joséphine and in her garden at Malmaison. Daughter of Atlas with whom Ulysses spent seven years.

Camaieux 16, **40**, 41

Camaieux Reversion 41

Cambronne. Before 1848. Very large, doubled, expanded vivid rose, shaded dark mauve-gray. Vigorous branching growth.

Camille Desmoulins. Before 1848. Large, double, rose-crimson. French revolutionist (1760-1794).

Camuzet Carnée. Before 1848. Gallica-China hybrid. Large, double, peach.

Camuzet Nouvelle. Before 1848. Gallica-China hybrid. Bright rose-crimson.

Canaris. Vétillard, France, 1826. Violet-purple.

Canary Island (Study name) 41

Candide. Descemet, France, 1820. Gallica-Centifolia hybrid. Small. Blush white. Voltaire's hero in novel of same name.

Canning. Parmentier, Belgium. Carmine.

Caprice de Zéphir. Hardy, France, 1823. An Agathe rose. Blush pink.

Capricorne 43

Captaine Williams 43

Captain Williams. See 'Captaine Williams'.

Caranjean. Before 1848. Large, double, pale lilac.

Cardinal Alberoni. Crimson.

Cardinal d'Ambroise. Crimson.

Cardinal de Bonnald. Parmentier, Belgium. Deep purple.

Cardinal de Cheverus. Robert, France, 1845. Large, full, compact, violet.

Cardinal de Chevreuse. Vibert, France. Violet.

Cardinal de Richelieu 15, **42**, 43

Cardon. Cardon. Deep purple with a brighter center.

Carmin Amoureux. Carmine.

Carmin Brillant. See 'Carmine Brilliante'.

Carmine Brilliante 43

Carmin Liséré. See 'La Majestueuse' [#2].

Carmin Royale. Before 1848. Large, full, compact, light crimson. A Gallica hybrid.

Carmosina. Calvert, France, before 1838. Medium, very full, crimson.

Carnation. van Eeden, Holland, before 1834.

Carné Parviflora. Lemeunier, France, 1826. Blush white.

Caroline Joly. Vibert, France, 1822.

Caroline Walner. Before 1848. Gallica-China hybrid. Double, cupped, pale rose-pink.

Carre de Boisjeloup. Before 1848. Gallica-China hybrid. Double, expanded, mauve-gray.

Casimir Bonjour. Crimson.

Casimir de Lavigne. Before 1834. Several later roses share this name. Named after a French poet.

Casimir Périer ('Casimir Perrier'). Savoureux, France, before 1838. Large, double, compact, cherry-crimson with bluish lilac circumference and mottled with blush. Upright growth.

Casimo Ridolphi. See 'Cosimo Ridolphi'.

Casseret Foncé. Deep carmine.

Catalonian. Before 1834.

Catherine de Medicis. Miellez, France, before 1834. Large, very full, crimson. Often proliferates, producing a bud in the center of the flower. Wife of Francis I. Arriving at the French court in 1553, might she have brought with her a few roses from Florence? The Medici interest in roses stemmed from at least the fifteenth century.

Catinat   43

Catulle. Vibert, France. Pink. Named after Catullus, Roman lyric poet (B.C. 84(?)-54).

Caura. Before 1900. Purple and violet blend.

Cécile Boireau. See 'Bizarre Marbré'.

Céleste. See 'Grande Sultane' [#3].

Celestial. Before 1848. Gallica-China hybrid. Large, full, cupped, crimson-rose blossoms, marbled and shaded crimson-purple.

Célestine ('Illustre Beauté'). Vibert, France, before 1838. Large, double, compact, well-formed, rosy blush blooms in clusters. Branching growth.

Céline d'Ortéga. Parmentier, Belgium. Clear lilac.

Celinette. Before 1848. Gallica-Centifolia hybrid. Medium, double, compact, pale blush. Almost white circumference. Upright growth.

Cellier. Salmon pink.

Cels Pleine. Carmine pink. Different from the below listed 'Rose Cels Pleine'.

Cerise d'Enghein. Holland. Deep rose.

Cerise d'Orlin. Loose semi-double, rich deep pink. Petals with a silvery reverse.

Cerise Superbe ('Cerise Superbissima'). Before 1846. Medium, very full, vivid cherry-crimson. Profuse bloom. Branching growth.

Cerisette la Jolie. See 'Surpasse Tout'.

Césare Beccaria   43

Chabrant. Violet blossoms.

Chambriere. Miellez, France. Pink.

Champion [#1]. Before 1834. Bright crimson.

Champion [#2]. Vibert, France, before 1848. Large, full, dark purple blooms mottled nearly black.

Chancellor of England ('Chancelier d'Angleterre' and also as simply 'Chancellor'). Calvert, France, before 1838. Medium, double, rich crimson, marbled purple.

Changeante ('Le Changeante'). Miellez, France, before 1838. Large, very full, crimson blooms, sometimes with white spots.

Chapeau Noir. Miellez, France, before 1848. Full, compact, crimson blossoms with darker violet shading.

Chapeau Rouge. Miellez, France. Purple.

Chapelain d'Aremberg   44

Chapelain d'Arenberg. See 'Chapelain d'Aremberg'.

Charlemagne. See 'President Dutailley'.

Charles Auguste (Sometimes as 'Charles Augustus'.) Paillard, 1824. Large, double, light pink aging to pale flesh color. Very thorny growth.

Charles de Mills   11, 16, 44, **45**

Charles Foucquier. Before 1848. Gallica-China hybrid. Double, globular, deep crimson with a lilac circumference.

Charles Lemayeux. Deep crimson.

Charles Lemoine. Lilac purple.

Charles Louis [#1]. Before 1848. Gallica-China hybrid. Large, double, cupped, rose-carmine blossom with a green button eye.

Charles Louis [#2]. Before 1848. Gallica-China hybrid. Small, full, compact, rose-blush.

Charles Martel. Parmentier, Belgium. Dark purple. Famous warrior defeated Arabs in 732 between Tours and Poitiers, led expeditions into Saxony, and was in all but name the sole king of the Franks.

Charles Mills. See 'Charles de Mills'.

Charles Quint   44

Charles Wills. See 'Charles de Mills'.

Charles X. See 'Bandeau de Soliman'.

Charlotte Corday. Blush white. Stabbed Marot to death during the French Revolution.

Charlotte de La Charme. Vibert, France, before 1838. Medium, full, pink, spotted. Small, glossy red hips.

Charmante Isidore. Boutigny, France, before 1834. Medium, very full, lilac-crimson, shaped and spotted with mauve-pink. Small upright growth.

Charmante Louise. Purple flowers.

Charmante Violette. Flesh pink.

Chaste Suzanne. Before 1848. Very large, full, cupped, blush.

Châteaubriand. Purple. French author and statesman (1768-1848).

Château de Namur   44

Chaucer   44

Chénédolé   44

Chérie. Lerouge, France, before 1834.

Chermesissimo Amplo. See 'Temple d'Apollon'.

Cherry. Before 1834.

Chévrier. Before 1848. Gallica-China hybrid. Violet-purple.

Chianti   16, **45**

Chloris   46

Chou. Pale pink.

Cicéro ('Cicéron'). Vibert, France, before 1846. Large, double, expanded, crimson blooms, shaded mauve. Vigorous upright growth. Roman orator and statesman.

Cicris Rose ('Crevalis', 'Crivalis'). Vibert, France, before 1838. Medium, very double, bright purplish violet.

Cinthie. Descemet, France. Crimson violet.

Cire d'Espangne. Miellez, France, before 1838. Medium, full, bright vivid crimson.

Cisaque de Sibérie. Holland. Purple with crimson center.

Claisigny. 1826. Large, very full, well-formed, velvety crimson blooms.

Clara ('Maximus'). Miellez, France, before 1834. Medium, full, vivid lilac-pink.

Clarinde. Lilac blooms.

Claris. Before 1834.

Clarisse Jolivet. Vibert, France, before 1848. Gallica-Centifolia hybrid. Large, double, white.

Clarisse Manson. Vibert, France, 1816.

Clédoxe. Before 1838. Gallica-Centifolia hybrid. Medium, dark crimson blooms with a high center.

Clélie. Before 1848. Gallica-Centifolia hybrid. Very large, full, expanded, clear blush pink. Vigorous upright growth.

Clémence Isaure. See 'Aimable Sophie'.

Clémentine. Vibert, France, before 1818. Medium, full, flesh pink. Sometimes spotted.

Clémentine Duval. Flesh pink, spotted.

Clémentine Joineaux ('La Somptuese'). Racine, France, before 1838. Large, double, pale clear rose-pink.

Cleo ('Clio'). Descemet, France, before 1813. In Joséphine's collection. Flesh pink. Daughter of Zeus; one of the nine Muses.

Cléobuline. Vibert, France, 1820.

Cléodone ('Cléodoxe'). Hardy, France. Deep pink.

Cléopâtra ('Cléopâtre'). Vibert, France, 1819. Gallica-Centifolia hybrid. Medium, double, compact, light salmon pink. Fragrant. Upright growth.

Clio. See 'Cleo'.

Clorinde. Before 1848. Large, double, compact, well-formed blossoms of soft purple-lilac with mauve shading and a crimson center.

Clothilde. Coquerel, France, 1867. Pale pink.

Clotilda. Before 1838. Medium, full, evenly colored soft pink. Glossy foliage. Wife of Clovis.

Clotilde. Noisette, France, 1827. Velvety crimson.

Clovis. Miellez, France. Pink flowers. Founder of the Frankish monarchy (466(?)-511).

Cocarde Pâle 46

Cocarde Rouge ('Grandeur Triomphante'). Vibert or Prévost, France, before 1838. Very large, full, compact, soft rose-pink. Pendulous growth. Large globular hips.

Cocarde Royale ('Grand Monarque'). Hardy, France, before 1813. Large, double, soft pink. In Joséphine's collection at Malmaison.

Cocard Jacobea. Belgium, 1824. Large, semi-double, crimson blossom with a large boss of stamens.

Coccinea Superba ('Vingt-neuf Julliet', 'Le 29 Julliet'). Before 1848. Gallica-China hybrid. Deep crimson. Large, double, compact with vivid crimson center.

Cochineal. Before 1846. Bright crimson.

Coerulescens Marmorata. V. Verdier, France, 1852. Mauve, marbled.

Coeur Aimable. Miellez, France. Purple.

Coeur Noir. Miellez, France. Blackish crimson.

Colette. Noisette, France, 1827. Medium, very full, velvety crimson blooms in clusters of three.

Colonel Coombes. Before 1848. Gallica-Centifolia hybrid. Very large, double, expanded, and well-formed blooms. Light crimson, shaded lilac and purple. Vigorous growth.

Colonel Fabvier ('Fabvier'). Laffay, France, 1832. Gallica-China hybrid. Large, double, cupped, vivid rose-pink.

Columella. See 'Columelle'.

Columelle 46

Commandant Beaurepaire. See 'Panachée d'Angers'.

Complicata 15, 16, 46, **47**

Comte Boula de Nanteuil. See 'Boule de Nanteuil'.

Comte de Colbert. Crimson blossoms with a violet border.

Comte de Flandre. Before 1848. Medium, full, cupped, dark crimson blossoms.

Comte de Lacépède. Before 1846. Large, double, rosy lilac blossoms.

Comte de Murinais. Before 1846. Very large, very full, cupped, slate-mauve blooms spotted rose and chocolate. Vigorous upright growth.

Comte d'Epernon. Flesh pink.

Comte de Roma. Before 1834.

Comte Foy de Rouen [#1] 48

Comte Foy de Rouen [#2] ('Admirable Panachée', 'Double Variegated Provins Rose'). Belgium, 1827. Variegated white and crimson.

Comtesse Almavia. Before 1848. Large, double, compact, well-formed, bright crimson. Upright growth.

Character in operas, one by Rossini; the other, Mozart.

Comtesse d'Alvilliers. Lilac-pink blossoms.

Comtesse de Baillet ('Nouveau Rose Marguerite'). 1827. Flesh pink.

Comtesse de Bedford. Crimson blooms.

Comtesse de Genlis. Vibert, France, 1817. Blush white.

Comtesse de Lacépède 48

Comtesse de Mélores.

Comtesse de Montalivet. Before 1848. Gallica-China hybrid. Medium, double, cupped, soft crimson blooms, shaded dark mauve.

Comtesse de Murinais. Robert, France, 1843. Clear pink.

Comtesse Plater. Before 1848. Gallica-China hybrid. Large, double, cupped, creamy white with a blush center.

Comte Walsch. Before 1846. Small, double, compact, rose-pink blooms mottled crimson and edged blush. Small upright growth.

Comus. Before 1848. Medium, full, cupped, rose-pink with a crimson center. Roman god of revelry and nocturnal entertainment.

Concard Pâle. Before 1813. In Joséphine's collection.

Conditorum 48

Congrès de Gand. Deep purple.

Conspicua. Before 1848. Gallica-China hybrid. Double, cupped, rose-crimson.

Constance. Before 1834.

Constance Spry 11, 48

Constantin ('Idalise'). Vibert, France, before 1838. Large, very double, evenly colored vivid deep pink. First Christian emperor of Rome.

Coq de Biez. Lilac-crimson.

Coq de Village. Purple blooms.

Coquelicot. 1820. Bright crimson.

Coquereau. Before 1848. Large, double, pink-veined crimson.

Cora 48

Coralie Ponctuée. Pink, spotted white.

Cordon Bleu ('Le Cordon Bleu', 'Pleine Lune', 'Full Moon Rose'). Prévost, France, before 1838. Medium, double, lilac-slate.

Cordon Bleu de Baltet ('Grande Bichonne'). Calvert, France. Light bright crimson.

Cordon Double. Clear pink.

Cordon Rouge. Deep pink.

Corine. Vibert, France, 1818. Small, full, convex, pale pink with white edges.

Corinne. Before 1848. Gallica-Centifolia hybrid. Mid-size, double, globular, rose-pink.

Cornelia. Crimson.

Cornélie [#1]. Garilland, France, before 1838. Large, double, convex, pink.

Cornélie [#2]. Prévost, France. Deep pink, bordered with lilac.

Coronation [#1]. Before 1846. Very double, well-formed blooms. Bright crimson. The older variety.

Coronation [#2]. Before 1846. Gallica-China hybrid. Double, compact, purple with bluish shading.

Corvisart. Laffay, France, 1825. Gallica-China hybrid. Double, cupped, pink.

Cosimo Ridolfi   **49**

Cottage Maid. See 'Perle des Panachées'.

Couleur à la Mode. Holland, before 1834. Bluish mauve.

Couleur de Brennus. Crimson.

Couleur de Mérise ('Rose Couleur de Mérise'). Vibert, France, before 1838. Large, semi-double, velvety bright rich purple flowers.

Couleur Excellente. Before 1834.

Couleur Lilas. Descemet, France. Lilac.

Coupe d'Amour. Laffay, France, before 1848. Gallica-China hybrid. Medium, double, cupped, pale pink.

Couronné d'Amour. Before 1848. Double, pale pink.

Couronné d'Ariane. Racine, France. Flesh pink.

Couronné de Brabant ('Rose Scris', 'Scris Rose'). Calvert, France, before 1838. Large, double, pale pink.

Couronné de Président. Before 1848. Large, full, crimson with a more vivid center.

Couronné des Roses. Before 1848. Medium, very full, deep purplish crimson.

Couronné des Rouges. Before 1834.

Couronnée. Clear violet.

Couronné Impériale ('La Superbe', 'Crown Impérial', 'Superbe' [#2]). Descemet, France, before 1834. Large, double, clear deep violet-pink with darker mauve shading. Reintroduced by Vibert.

Couronné Pourpre. Before 1834.

Couronné Royale ('Empereur Couronné', 'Mme. Roland' [#1], 'Roi Couronné'). Medium, double, convex, bright lilac-pink with bluish tones. Compact upright growth.

Courtin ('Rose Courtin'). Cartier, France, 1824. Gallica-Centifolia hybrid. Large, very double, flesh pink.

Couture. See 'Auzou'.

[Note: In various references, the following roses may be found as either *Cramoisi* or *Cramoisie*.]

Cramoisi. Crimson and violet.

Cramoisi Brilliant. Crimson.

Cramoisi des Alpes   49

Cramoisi Éblouissant   49

Cramoisie Enflammé. Before 1846.

Cramoisie Impériale. Before 1834.

Cramoisie Incomparable. Before 1834.

Cramoisie Nouvelle. Before 1834.

Cramoisie sans Pareille. Before 1834.

Cramoisi Nuancé. Vibert, France, 1822. Crimson, shaded.

Cramoisi Picoté   16, **50**, 51

Cramoisi Ponctuée ('Herminie' [#7]). Prévost, France. Medium, full, crimson, spotted.

Cramoisi Royal. Descemet, France.

Cramoisissimo Amplo. See 'Temple d'Apollon'.

Cramoisi Triomphant. Before 1846. Mauve-gray, finely spotted crimson. In Joséphine's collection.

Cramoisi Violet. Vibert, France, 1819.

Crépue à Feuilles Ondulées. Descemet, France. Purple-crimson.

Creralio. Calvert, France. Deep purple-pink.

Crested Provence. Pink with a paler border.

Crevalis. See 'Cicris Rose'.

Crivalis. See 'Cicris Rose'.

Croix d'Honneur. Prévost, France, before 1838. Small, double, bright crimson.

Crown Impérial. See 'Couronne Impériale'.

Crown of Ariadne. Before 1838. Large, double, flesh pink.

Cumberland. See 'Grande Sultane' [#2] and comment under 'La Belle Sultane'.

Cupid ('Cupidon'). Miellez, France, before 1848. Large, full, cupped, delicate flesh pink.

Cupidon de Cumberland. Prévost, France. Clear pink blooms.

Curé de Biez. Lilac-pink.

Cuvier. Vibert, France, 1843. Large, full, cupped rose-pink, spotted white.

Cybele. Racine, France, before 1838. Large, double, dark purple. Ancient Asian goddess; Greek and Roman goddess of agriculture, who was represented with a towered crown on her head, and during whose festivals, roses were scattered.

Cymodée. Before 1848. Large, double, cupped, deep crimson, shaded with scarlet.

Cymodocée. Laffay, France, before 1848. Gallica-China hybrid. Large, double, delicate rose color.

Cynthie [#1]   51

Cynthie [#2]. Deep lilac-crimson. Another name for the moon goddess, Diana.

Cyparisse. Before 1848. Medium, full, compact, rose-crimson shaded with mauve. Branching growth. Youth transformed by Apollo into a cypress tree.

Cyrus. Before 1846. Large, cupped, lilac-rose. King and founder of the Persian Empire, (?-B.C. 529).

d'Aguesseau   51

Damascena Mutabilis. See 'Belle de Cels'.

Dames. Before 1834.

Dames du Luxemburg. Before 1834.

Danae [#1]. Before 1834. Mythological beauty.

Danae [#2]. Robert, France, 1854. Violet-pink.

Dandigne de la Blanchaie. Before 1848. Gallica-China hybrid. Double, deep gray-purple with a crimson center.

Daphné [#1]   51

Daphné [#2]. See 'Nouveau Triomphe'. This is the 'Daphné' described by Gore, not the Hybrid Bourbon in Paul.

D'Arago. Pale pink.

Darius. Deep crimson. King of Persia.

D'Assas. 1844. Medium, full, deep violet spotted.

Daubenton. Before 1848. Very large, double, cupped, rose shaded mauve-gray. Vigorous upright growth.

Dauphine. France, 1814. Clear, rosy pink.

Decandolle. Before 1848. Gallica-China hybrid. Large, semi-double, cupped, vivid crimson.

De Cornouailles. Sommesson. Violet and lilac.

De Gontille. Pink blossoms.

Déjanire. Robert, France, before 1838. Medium, double, soft pink.

De Jéricho. Deep pink.

De Jessaint. Girardon, France. Deep violet.

De La Maître d'École. See 'Rose du Maître d'École'.

De La Reine. See 'Passe Princesse'.

Delaunay. Pink.

Delicate. Dubourg, France. Cerise-pink, variegated lilac.

Délices de Flandres ('Delight of Flanders'). Miellez, France, before 1838. Gallica-Centifolia hybrid. Large, loosely double, flesh pink.

Delille [#1] ('Rose Delille'). Vibert, France, 1822. Bright clear crimson.

Delille [#2]. Vibert, France, 1836. Medium, double, purple spotted with violet.

Delisiosa. Before 1834.

Delphine. Before 1848. Cupped, purplish crimson.

Delphine Gay. Vibert, France. Light crimson.

De Messine. Sommesson, 1823. Pale pink blooms.

De Misson. Deep rose.

De Naple. Before 1834.

De Nicolai. Before 1834.

De Pronville. Flesh pink blossoms.

Désaix. Vibert, France, 1844. Mid-size, double, deep crimson-purple.

Des Alpes Simple. Flesh pink and lilac.

Desbrosses. See 'Belle de Desbrosses'.

Descartes. Vibert, France, 1846. Gallica-China hybrid. Mid-size, double, velvety violet-purple. French philosopher.

Descemet. See 'Agathe Parfaite'.

Deschamps. Charpentier. Pink.

De Schelfhout. See 'Rose de Schelfhout'.

De Schelfont. See 'Rose de Schelfhout'.

Desfontaines. Cartier, France, before 1838. Medium, loosely double, well-formed, vivid carmine blooms.

Deshoulieres ('Mme. Deshoulieres'). Belgium, 1812. Medium, double, compact, evenly colored cherry-rose. Upright growth. Perhaps with some Damask in parentage.

Désirée. Joly, France, 1835. Pink blossoms.

Désirée Parmentier   52, **53**

Des Parfumeurs. See 'Rosier des Parfumeurs'.

De Ste. Aldegonde. Parmentier, Belgium. Pink shaded.

Deuil. Prévost, France. Lilac blossoms.

Deuil de Maréchal Mortier ('Maréchal Mortier'). Before 1848. A Gallica-China hybrid. Large, double, cupped blossoms of velvety purple-crimson. Base of white petals.

De van Eeden ('Rosier van de Eeden'). van Eeden, Holland, 1810. Purple-violet. In Joséphine's collection at Malmaison.

Devigne. Before 1848. Gallica-Centifolia hybrid. Medium, double, compact, well-formed, rose-blush blooms. Branching growth.

Diadème de Flore-Alix (Alix Diadème de Flore'). Sommesson, 1825. Flesh pink with a pale lilac border. Similar to one below but with larger blossoms.

Diadème de Flore-Ancien ('Ancien Diadème de Flore'). Vibert, France. Lilac-pink, mid-size, double blossoms.

Diadème Superb. Before 1846. Small, double, ranunculus-form blooms. Vivid crimson.

Diane. Holland. Purple with a crimson center.

Diane de Poitiers. Before 1834.

Diderot. Crimson, shaded deeper. Prolific French author (1713-1784).

Dido. Before 1848. Large, double, cupped, deep rose color with crimson center. Upright growth. Mythological Queen of Carthage.

Didon. See 'Agathe Parfaite'.

Docteur Billiard. See 'Beauté of Billiard'.

Docteur Dielthim. Before 1848. Very large, double, compact, well-formed, rose-colored blooms, shaded purple. Vigorous branching growth.

Docteur Guérin. Vibert, France, before 1848. Gallica-China hybrid. Large, double, purple-violet.

Dometille Beccard   52

Doña Sol   52

Don de l'Amitié. See 'Nouveau Triomphe'.

Don des Dames. Before 1834.

Donna Francisca. Before 1848. Vivid crimson marbled with lilac.

Dorothée [#1] ('Victoire de Bragance', 'Victory of Braganza'). Hardy, France, before 1838. Medium, full, compact, convex, cherry-crimson blooms.

Dorothée [#2] ('Dosithée'). Noisette, France, before 1838. Crimson, marbled crimson-purple. Branching growth.

Dosithée. See 'Dorothée' [#2].

Double Brique   52

Double Variegated Provins Rose. See 'Comte Foy de Rouen' [#2].

Down. Pale pink.

Dragon. Before 1834.

Dubois Dessaussais. Vibert, France, 1842. Pale pink.

Duc d'Angoulême [#1]   52

Duc d'Angoulême [#2] ('Duchesse d'Angoulême' [#2], and possibly, 'Duc de Baviere' [#2]). Most often listed as a Centifolia but this rose could have been a Centifolia x Gallica cross. Double, bright deep clear pink.

Duc d'Anhalt. Parmentier, Belgium. Dark purple.

Duc d'Aremberg   55

Duc de Bassano. Crimson and violet, marbled white.

Duc de Bavière [#1]. See Duc d'Angoulême [#1].

Duc de Bavière [#2]. See 'Duc d'Angoulême' [#2]. Possibly a Centifolia. Deep pink.

Duc de Beauford ('Duke of Beaufort'). Belgium, 1825. Medium, flesh pink and violet. Well-formed, very full blossoms.

Duc de Berry. ('Roi d'Angleterre' [#1]). Vibert, France, before 1834. Double, mid-size blossoms of dark violet-purple.

Duc de Bordeaux   55

Duc de Fitzjames   55

Duc de Guiche   **56**

Duc de Leuchtenberg. Before 1834.

Duc de Lorraine. Mauve and crimson flowers.

Duc de Luxembourg. White with a pink center.

Duc de Nemours. Robert, France. Lilac, shaded pink.

Duc d'Enghien. Parmentier, Belgium. Cerise and violet.

Duc de Northumberland. Vétillard, France. Violet.

Duc de Richelieu ('Richelieu'). Verdier, France, 1843. Gallica-China hybrid. Large, double, compact, lilac-rose. Another rose named after Cardinal Richelieu.

Enfant de France Nouveau ('Tout Aimable'). Pelletier, France, before 1838. Small, full, crimson.

Enfant de l'Ouragan. Pink.

Enfant du Nord. Before 1848. Medium, double, compact, well-formed, rosy crimson blooms. Vigorous branching growth.

Eponine. Before 1838. Medium, very double, mauve-crimson, shaded crimson.

Erdelinde. Toutain, France, 1824. Violet pink.

Erigone. Vibert, France, 1822. Mid-size, double, light clear crimson-purple.

Ermite. Miellez, France. Purple.

Ernest. Bachelier. Crimson with a violet sheen.

Ernest Ferray. Before 1848. Gallica-China hybrid. Large, full, crimson.

Ernestine. Miellez. Deep pink.

Erythrine. Vétillard, France, 1827. Deep crimson.

Estelle   60

Esther   60

Eucharis   60

Eugène. Boutigny, France, 1825. Medium, double, round, pale lilac-rose.

Eugène de Barbier. Before 1848. Large, double, compact, crimson.

Eugène Janvier. Medium, full, rich rose-colored flowers, paling to lilac.

Eugène Maille. Boutigny, France, before 1838. Very large, full blossoms of vivid pink.

Eugène Napoléon. Before 1848. Large, double, well-formed, vivid rose-crimson, tinged bright purple. Branching growth.

Eugènie. See 'Nouveau Triomphe'.

Eulalia Le Brun. See 'Eulalie Lebrun'.

Eulalie. Miellez, France, before 1834. Pink, striped.

Eulalie Lebrun   60, **61**

Euphrasie. Vibert, France, 1845. Mid-size, double, rich rose color. Delicately spotted.

Euphrosine. Vibert, France, 1826. Gallica-China hybrid. Light clear pink. One of the Graces.

Euphrosine L'Élégante. See 'Euphrosyne L'Élégante'.

Euphrosyne L'Élégante   62

Euridice. Before 1834. Crimson.

Eurydice. Before 1848. Large, full, pale rose. Wife of Orpheus.

Eutaxie. Noisette, France, 1827. Crimson blooms.

Eva Corinna. Feast, USA, 1843. Tentative identification at Roseraie de l'Haÿ. One of the few U.S. Gallica hybrids to find its way into European collections.

Eveline   62

Évêque d'Angers ('Montault'). Before 1848. Gallica-China hybrid. Large, double, deep crimson.

Ex Albo Aurantia. Before 1834.

Ex Albo Inermis Violacea. Descemet, France. Lilac.

Ex Albo Rosea. See 'Lee' [#1].

Ex Albo Violacea. Noisette, France, before 1834. Very large, semi-double, vivid lilac-rose.

Ex Albo Violacea Crispa. Descemet, France. Lilac.

Eynard. Laffay, France, before 1848. Gallica-China hybrid. Medium, double, cupped, pale cherry-crimson. Closely set, twisted petals.

Fabvier. See 'Colonel Fabvier'.

Fanny Bias   62

Fanny Chatenay. Before 1834.

Fanny Essler   62

Fanny Geefs. Parmentier, Belgium. Deep purple crimson.

Fanny Marschall. Deep lilac.

Fanny Parissot. See 'Fanny Bias'.

Fanny Pavetot   62

Fatime. See 'Agathe Fatime'.

Faustine. Vibert, France. Purple-violet.

Favorite des Dames. Before 1834.

Favorite Mignon. Before 1834.

Favorite Pourpre. Before 1834.

Félicie ('Petite Renoncule', 'Sultane Favorite', 'Petite Renoncule Violette'). Vibert, France, 1823. Small, very double, dark purple-crimson to violet. 'Sultane Favorite' is sometimes attributed to Miellez. One of many contradictory attributions involving Miellez's roses.

Félicité. Before 1834.

Felix. Parmentier. Deep rose.

Fénelon. Before 1838. Wine-crimson, spotted. French prelate and writer (1651-1715).

Fenon Rouge Agathe. Light clear crimson.

Ferdinand de Buck   63

Ferdinand the First. Laffay, France, before 1848. Gallica-China hybrid. Very large, full, purple-lilac.

Festina. Before 1834.

Feu Amoureux. See 'Feu d'Amour'.

Feu Brillant [#1]. Vibert, France. Carmine.

Feu Brillant [#2]. Prévost, France, before 1838. Very large, loosely double, vivid bright crimson. Vigorous upright growth.

Feu d'Amour ('Feu Amoureux'). Before 1834. Clear lilac-purple.

Feu de Buck. See 'Ferdinand de Buck'.

Feu de Moskowa. Before 1848. Mid-sized, cupped, well-formed, bright rose blooms, shaded purple.

Feu de Vesta ('Vesta'). Coquerel, France, before 1838. Large, semi-double, velvety bright crimson.

Feu Non Rouge. Before 1813. In Joséphine's collection.

Feu Panaché. Prévost, France, before 1838. Small, very full, bright crimson.

Feu Turc. Miellez, France, before 1838. Medium, well-formed, bright crimson, tinged purple.

Fidèle. See 'La Fidèle'.

Fidelia. Prévost, France, before 1838. Medium, double, light bright pink.

Fimbriata à Pétals Frangées ('à Pétals Frangées'). Jacques, France, 1831. Gallica-China hybrid. Mid-size, very full, bright crimson with fringed petals, resembling those of a carnation.

Fina Soestmans. Flesh pink flowers.

Fintelmans. Germany. Deep dark crimson.

Flamboyant. Descemet, France, before 1834. Small, full, deep rich purple. Vivid crimson center.

Flammé du Vésuve. Miellez, France. Vivid crimson.

Flandres. Before 1834.

Flavia. Descemet, France.

Fleur d'Amour. Before 1846. Medium to large, very full, expanded, brilliant violet-crimson. Upright growth.

Fleur de Passerose. Pelletier, France, 1827. Pale pink and blush.

Fleur de Pommier ('Fleur des Pommes'). Holland, before 1834. Medium, full, soft pink, evenly colored.

Fleurs Bombées. Noisette, France, 1827. Pink.

Fleurs Comprimées. Vibert, France, 1822.

Fleurs de Passion. Pelletier, France, 1827. Flesh pink with a blush border.

Fleurs de Pelletier 63

Flora. Vibert, France, before 1834. Mid-size, full, flesh pink. Roman goddess of spring and flowers.

Flora M'Ivor ('Flora McIvor'). Laffay, France, before 1848. Gallica-China hybrid. Large, double, cupped, pale lilac-pink with a blush circumference.

Flora Prévost. Pink.

Flora Rubra. Before 1834.

Florentine. Before 1834.

Fontenelle. Trébucien, France, before 1838. Large, double, expanded, deep mauve-rose, spotted with blush. Upright growth.

Forges de Vulcain. Miellez, France. Purple. Vulcan, Roman deity of fire and metalwork.

Fornarina 63

Fortunée. Before 1834.

Foucheaux. See 'Rose Foucheaux'.

Fouchér. Vibert, France, before 1838. Large, double, soft pink. Thornless.

Fox. Before 1848. Large, full, compact, purple. Mottled.

Francis Foucquier 63

Francofurtana. See 'Empress Joséphine'.

François Foucquier. See 'Francis Foucquier'.

Frankfort Rose. See 'Empress Joséphine'.

Franklin. Before 1846. Large, full, cupped, rich rose-crimson, shaded mauve. Branching growth.

Friedlanderiana. Gallica-China hybrid. Single, vivid rose-pink.

Fulgens. Vibert, France. Bright pale rose.

Full Flowering Juno. Before 1838. Medium, very full, rich rose color. Profuse bloom in clusters.

Full Hervey Rose. Before 1838. Large, very double, vivid claret-crimson. Petals rolled in the center.

Full Moon Rose. See 'Cordon Bleu'.

Gabina. Calvert, France, before 1838. Medium, full, spherical blossoms of light purple.

Gaillarde Marbrée ('Noire Couronnée'). Prévost, France, before 1813. Medium, full, velvety violet-purple, marbled crimson. Foliage narrow, often variegated.

Galatée. Parmentier, France, before 1838. Clear pink. Nymph of Greek fable.

Galien. Before 1848. Gallica-China hybrid. Very large, double, globular, rich crimson, aging to lilac-rose. Marbled with blush pink.

Galilée. Robert and Moreau, France. Lilac, spotted.

Gallica Alba. Blush white.

Gallica Maheka. See 'La Belle Sultane'.

Gallica Maxima Gigantea ('Louis XVIII' [#1]). Prévost, France, before 1834. Very large, loosely double, pale pink.

Gallica Mexica Aurantia. See 'Tricolore' [#1].

Gallica Vermillon. France, 1823. Very small, very doubled, soft pink. Compact, small growth.

Gallica Versicolor. See 'Gallique Panachée'.

Gallique Panachée ('La Rubanée' [#1], 'La Villageoise', 'Gallica Versicolor'). Prévost, France, before 1836. Semi-double, large white blooms, striped deep pink.

Gallique Presque Blanc. Lilac-flesh, bordered blush.

Ganganelli ('Gandanelli'). Lahaye, France. Lilac-pink.

Garilland. Vibert, France. Pale rose.

Garnet. Before 1834.

Gassendi. Hardy, France, 1827. Very large, very double, well-formed flowers of a rich rose color. French philosopher and scientist (1592-1655).

Gazella. Deep rose-pink. Different from 'Gazelle'.

Gazelle 63

Général Allard. Laffay, France, 1835. Gallica-China hybrid. Mid-size, very double, globular, rose-carmine. Occasional rebloom.

Général Bernard. Before 1834. Gallica-China hybrid. Medium, double, cupped, mauve with a crimson center. Marbled with slate-purple.

Général Bertrand [#1]. Before 1848. Cupped mauve-purple.

Général Bertrand [#2]. Vibert, France, 1845. Medium, very full, white blooms with lilac and crimson stripes.

Général Changarnier. Laffay, France, 1847. Gallica-China hybrid. Large, double, purple-crimson.

Général Christiany. Before 1848. Gallica-China hybrid. Large, full, cupped, light crimson.

Général Damrémont. Portemer, France. Purple and mauve.

Général Dausménil. Before 1848. Gallica-China hybrid. Large, double, globular, purple-violet.

Général de Bréa. Purple flowers.

Général Désaix. Boutigny, before 1838. Medium, double, rich pink with a paler circumference.

Général Donadieu. Before 1846. Double, compact, bright flesh pink.

Général Evain. Parmentier, Belgium. Dark crimson.

Général Foy [#1]. Pelletier, France, 1827. Very large, double, cupped, rich purple-rose with a brighter center. Gallica-Centifolia hybrid?

Général Foy [#2]. Vibert, France, 1845. Medium, double, purple, spotted dark violet.

Général Jacqueminot. Laffay, France, 1846. Gallica-China hybrid. Large, double, rich purple shaded crimson. Vigorous, upright growth. There is a later, more famous rose by the same name.

Général Junot. Purple blooms.

Général Klèber ('Klèber'). Before 1848. Gallica-China hybrid. Medium, double, cupped, deep purple-crimson aging to violet. This is neither the Moss rose nor the later Hybrid Perpetual by this name.

Général Lafayette ('Lafayette'). Before 1846. Medium, double, cupped, crimson blossoms, shaded purple. Branching growth and profuse bloom. A French statesman and military leader who distinguished himself in the American Revolution.

Général Lemarque ('Lemarque'). Before 1848. Gallica-China hybrid. Mid-size, very full, very dark velvety crimson-purple.

Général Lery. Pale pink.

Général Moreau 63

Général Pajol. Before 1834. Gallica-China hybrid. Medium, double, bright peach-pink.

Genevieve. Before 1834. Crimson.

Genoise. Before 1834.

Gentil ('Les Trois Mages', 'Les Mages', 'Rose de Gentil', 'The Three Magi'). Gentil (?), 1823. Medium, very full, convex, rich vivid rose-pink. Gallica-Centifolia hybrid. Gentil as hybridizer may have been an historical error, misinterpretation of 'Rose de

Gentil', which more likely refers to the importance of the biblical story: the moment Christ was revealed to the Gentiles.

Georges Vibert   **64**, 65

George the Fourth ('George IV'). Rivers, England, 1820. Gallica-China hybrid. Large, double, cupped, deep velvety purple-crimson. Purple-tinged foliage. Vigorous tall growth.

Georgette Mary. Laffay, France. Deep rose. Obtained from Parmentier of Belgium.

Georgina Mars. Savoureux, France, before 1838. Small, very double, well-formed, light vivid pink, striped white.

Gerardon. Before 1848. Large, double violet-crimson.

Gertrude Bernard. Noisette, France, 1827. Crimson.

Giant. Before 1834.

Gil Blas   65

Gildippa. Miellez, France. Crimson.

Girondet. Carmine blossoms.

Giselle. Vibert, France, 1843. Medium, double, rose-pink spotted.

Globe Blanc. See 'Boule de Neige' [#1].

Globe Céleste. Before 1838. Gallica-Centifolia hybrid. Very large, double, well-formed flesh pink blooms.

Globe White Hip. See 'Boule de Neige' [#2].

Gloire de Colmar. Before 1848. Gallica-China hybrid. Compact, deep crimson-purple.

Gloire de Couline. Before 1848. Gallica-China hybrid. Large, double, cupped, crimson blooms, shaded carmine.

Gloire de France   11, 16, 65

Gloire des Agathes. Before 1845. Agathe rose. Lilac-rose.

Gloire des Héllènes ('La Nubienne'). Laffay, France, 1825. Gallica-China hybrid. Medium, double, cupped, rich velvety slate-purple.

Gloire des Jardins   65

Gloire des Pouprés ('Validatum'). Before 1838. Large, very doubled, violet-purple.

Gloria Mundi. See 'La Plus Belle des Violettes'.

Gloria Nigrorum. Calvert, France. Deep purple-violet.

Gloria Rubrorum. Before 1834. Deep crimson blossoms.

Gloriette   65

Glory of France. See 'Gloire de France'.

Glory of the Gardens Pallagi. See 'Ne Plus Ultra' [#2].

Glycère. Vibert, France, 1845. Gallica-Centifolia hybrid. Medium, double, blush-colored blossoms with flesh shading.

Godecharles. Parmentier, Belgium. Deep pink.

Goliath. Girardon, France, before 1838. Gallica-Centifolia hybrid. Large, deep pink blossoms.

Gonatre. Before 1848. Mid-size, double, compact blooms. Light bright carmine occasionally mottled purple. Branching growth.

Gonsalve   65

Goût du Jour. Miellez, France. Pink.

Gracieuse ('Gracieuse de St. Cloud'). Miellez, France, before 1834. Pink.

Gracilis. Vibert, France, before 1834. White striped.

Graim Dosk. Before 1848. Large, double, compact, well-formed, deep purple with a vivid rose-crimson center. Vigorous, upright growth.

Grain d'Or ('Green d'Hoor', 'Grain d'Hort', 'Graindhost' and possibly as 'Graim Dosk'). Prévost, France, before 1838. Medium, very double, compact, rich velvety crimson, shaded and mottled purple. Profuse bloom and upright growth.

Granats Pomme. Before 1834.

Grand Apollon. Brussels, Belgium, 1824. Very large, full, violet.

Grand Ardoise. Hardy, France. Violet and white.

Grand Clovis. See 'Aldégonde' [#2].

Grand Conde. See 'Aldégonde' [#1].

Grand Corneille. See 'Cramoisi des Alpes'.

Grand Couronnée. See 'Belle de Cels'.

Grand Cramoisi   66

Grand Cramoisi Superbe. Before 1834.

Grande Agathe. Before 1834. Very full, blush white with white center.

Grande Agathe Nouvelle ('Isabelle'). Vibert, France, before 1834. Flesh pink, shaded with crimson.

Grande Bichonne. See 'Cordon Bleu de Baltet'.

Grande Brique. Before 1838. Gallica-Centifolia hybrid. Very large, full, peony-form blossoms. Clear lilac-pink.

Grande Engheinoise. Parmentier, Belgium. Bright pink.

Grande Esther. See 'Esther'.

Grande et Belle [#1]   66

Grande et Belle [#2]. Purple-pink.

Grande Henriette. See 'L'Enchanteresse'.

Grande Junon. van Eeden, Holland, before 1834.

Grande Merveilleuse. Vibert, France, before 1838. Gallica-Centifolia hybrid. Large, double, pale pink.

Grande Obscurité. See 'Passe Velours'.

Grande Renommée. See 'Belle de Cels'.

Grande Renoncule   66

Grandes Divinites ('Pourpre sans Aiquillons', 'Pourpre sans Épines'). Vibert, France, 1827. Medium, full, pinkish purple. Thornless.

Grandes Feuilles. Lelieur. Deep pink.

Grande Souveraine. Vibert, France, 1825. Large, loosely double, soft pink.

Grandesse Royale. See 'Passe Princesse'.

Grande Sultane [#1] ('Le Grand Sultan'). Descemet, France, 1813. Flesh pink.

Grande Sultane [#2] ('Cumberland'). Prévost, France. A Gallica-Centifolia hybrid. Semi-double. Light bright pink.

Grande Sultane [#3] ('Céleste', 'Grand Turban'). Calvert, France, before 1838. Very large, double, pale flesh pink. Light green foliage.

Grande Sultane [#4] ('Agathe Pyramidale Agréable'). Robert, France. Bright silky pink.

Grandeur. See 'La Grandeur'.

Grandeur Royale. See 'Passe Princesse'.

Grandeur Triomphante. See 'Cocarde Rouge'.

Grande Violette Claire. Violet-purple.

Grandidier ('Rose Grandidier'). Doubourg, France, 1826. Large, very double, well-formed blossoms. Violet-carmine.

Grandissima. See 'Louis Philippe' [#1].

Grand Maculée. See 'Aigle Brun Maculé'.

Grand Mogul ('Le Grand Mogul'). Prévost, France, before 1834. Medium, very full, rich vivid violet-crimson.

Grand Monarque. See 'Cocarde Royale'.

Grand Obscurité. See 'Passe Velours'.

Grand Papa ('Grandpapa'). Before 1838. Medium, very double, velvety purple, shaded crimson and occasionally mottled. Vigorous, branching growth.

Grand Pivoine de Lille. See 'Le Grand Triomphe'.

Grand Pompadour. See 'Pourpre Charmant'.

Grand Royale. See 'Passe Princesse'.

Grand St. Francis. See 'Lustre d' Eglise'.

Grand Sultan 66

Grand Triomphe. See 'Le Grand Triomphe'.

Grand Turban. See 'Grande Sultane' [#3].

Great English. Before 1834. Crimson.

Green d'Hoor. See 'Grain d'Or'.

Grenadine. Joly, France, 1835. Deep crimson blooms.

Grillony. Robert, France, before 1848. Gallica-China hybrid. Very large, very double, mauve.

Gris Cendre Petite. Ashen pink.

Groot Voorst. Before 1846. Large violet, spotted.

Gros Chalons ('Pourpre de Tyr'). Before 1838. Medium, doubled, evenly colored purplish rose.

Gros Fruit. France. Purple flowers.

Gros Major. Prévost, France, before 1838. Large, very double, bright crimson.

Gros Provins Panaché 66

Gros Sans Épines. Bright clear violet.

Grosse Cerise 66

Grosse Hollande ('Rosa Élongata'). Vibert, France, before 1834. Gallica-Centifolia hybrid. Medium, double, pale pink.

Grotius. Lilac-crimson. Dutch statesman and writer.

Guerin de Donai ('Guerin's Gift'). Before 1846. Large, full, well-formed blooms of bright rose shaded with violet. Vigorous, branching growth. Perhaps the same as 'Guerin', a Gallica-China hybrid by Vibert.

Guillaume Tell ('William Tell'). Before 1846. Very large, full compact, well-formed deep rose-pink with a blush border.

Guindal. Deep pink.

Habit Pourpre Foucée Étrangère. Before 1834.

Haddington 66

Hébé [#1]. Vibert, France, before 1838. Gallica-Centifolia hybrid. Semi-double, rich pink to pale crimson. Greek goddess of youth.

Hébé [#2]. Vibert, France, 1843. Gallica-China hybrid. Large, double, cupped, pale flesh pink.

Hector 66

Hélène. Miellez, France. Deep crimson.

Hélène de Jobkowitz. Crimson.

Heliodore Daullé. Crimson blossoms.

Heliodore Dober. Large, full, globular, dark crimson, edged bright crimson.

Héloïse [#1]. Vibert, France, before 1813. In Joséphine's collection. Flesh pink. Appears to have originally been from Holland, perhaps from van Eeden.

Héloïse [#2]. Lerouge, France. Purple-maroon.

Helvetia 66

Helvetius. Desprez, France. Crimson.

Hennequin. Desprez, France. Deep crimson.

Henri de Buck. Deep pink blooms.

Henriette 67

Henriette Blanche Double. Before 1834.

Henriette Grande Agathe. Cerise-pink.

Henri Foucquier. See 'Henri Fouquier'.

Henri Fouquier 67

Henri Lemain. Carmine.

Henri IV. Calvert, France. Crimson purple. Probably the same as 'Henry IV'.

Henry IV. See 'Adèle Heu'.

Henri V. Deep pink.

Henrion de Pansey. Before 1848. Large, double, purple.

Hera. Before 1834. Greek equivalent of Juno.

Hercule. Miellez, France, before 1844. Deep pink. Very fragrant, large, and very double. Hero of classical myth.

Herminie [#7]. See 'Cramoisi Ponctuée'. This rose is listed in *Nom de Roses*; the first six are not listed, nor described. Different from the 'Belle Herminie's.

Hermione. 1818. Pink. From Greek myth, wife of Cadmus; From Shakespeare, wife of King Leontes.

Hersilie. Before 1846. Mid-size, double, rose-pink blooms, spotted white. Gallica-China hybrid.

Hertford. Before 1834.

Hervy. Prévost, France, before 1838. Large, double, flattened, crimson blooms.

Hervy à Fleurs Pleines. Hardy, France. Lilac purple.

Heureuse Surprise. France, before 1846. Very large, double, bright rose-colored blooms, shaded with crimson and purple. Vigorous, upright growth.

Hildegarde. Noisette, France, 1827. Crimson with bluish tones.

Hippocrates. Before 1848. Gallica-China hybrid. Large, very full, cupped, rich crimson, striped rose-lilac. Greek physician, "Father of Medicine."

Hippolyte 67

Hispida. Before 1834.

Honneur de Flandre. Miellez, France, before 1848. Large, double, globular, lilac-purple. Upright growth.

Honneur de Montmorency. Before 1848. Gallica-China hybrid. Large, double, expanded rich crimson-purple. Branching growth.

Honneur des Jardins. Miellez, France. Deep crimson.

Honorine. Vibert, 1818. Pink blooms.

Honorine d'Esquermes. Miellez, France, before 1838. Large, double, flat, light crimson, marbled purple.

Hooker's Seedling. Before 1848. Small, double, compact, pale flesh pink. Vigorous, compact, upright growth.

Horace Vernet. Before 1848. Large double rose-pink. A French painter.

Hortense. Prévost, France. Flesh pink.

Hortense de Beauharnais 68

Hortensia. Miellez, France, before 1838. A Gallica-Centifolia hybrid. Large, full, hydrangea-pink.

Hospitalière ('L'Hospital', 'L'Hospitalière'). Robert, France, 1852. Medium, double, rich rose-pink, spotted light crimson.

Hundred-leaved Provins. Joly, France, before 1838.

Hundred-leaved Rose of Auteuil. Before 1838. Large, doubled, rose-colored. Outer petals often spotted.

Hungarian Rose. See 'Conditorum'.

Hybrida Nova. Descemet, France, before 1834. Carmine with a paler border.

Hybride Illustre. Before 1834.

Hypacia. See 'Hypathia'.

Hypathia 68

Hypatia. See 'Hypathia'.

Idalise. See 'Constantin'.

Idéalisée. Deep crimson blossoms.

Ildefonse. Noisette. France, 1827. Very large, very double, rich violet-pink. Vigorous growth with long flower stalks.

Illustre. See 'La Glorieuse' [#1].

Illustre Beauté. See 'Célestine'.

Illustre Champion. Before 1848. Very double, compact, deep purple-crimson.

Illustre en Beauté. Before 1838. Gallica-Centifolia hybrid. Medium, full, carmine.

Impératrice. Before 1834. Bluish tones.

Impératrice de Hollande ('Roi de Pays-Bas'). Before 1848. Gallica-Centifolia hybrid. Large, doubled, and cupped, brilliant pink.

Impératrice de Russie. Pean, France, before 1838. Gallica-Centifolia hybrid. Large, very full, well-formed, soft pink blossoms.

Impériale. Before 1834. Striped blossoms.

Impériale è Plumet. Pale pink.

Incomparable   69

Incomparable d'Auteuil. Laffay, France. Pink with a crimson center.

Incomparable de Lille ('L'Incomparable de Lille'). Prévost, France, before 1838. Large, full, pale flesh pink.

Incomparable de Luxemburg. Before 1834.

Incomparable Pourpre. Before 1846. Dark purple, mottled.

Incomparable Violette. Before 1846. Violet. Tall growth.

Inconnu. Deep pink. Indeed unknown!

Ines de Castro. Before 1848. Gallica-Centifolia hybrid. Medium, double, pale flesh pink.

Infanta de Asturias. Spain. Pale pink.

Infante. Before 1848. Large, double, rose-pink.

Infernal. Before 1834.

Inflexible. Purple flowers.

Insigne Destécles ('Isigne Destékles'). Before 1846. Medium, double, lilac-rose, marbled white. Branching growth.

Interessante ('L'Interessante'). Prévost, France, before 1838. Mid-size, double, strongly colored mauve-purple blossoms.

Invincible   69

Iphigénie. Vibert, France, 1820. Pink spotted. Daughter of Agamemnon and Clytemnestra. Subject of Greek tragedies; of Racine; 1779 Gluck opera.

Ipsilanté   69

Irena. Brilliant pink.

Irene. Laffay, France, before 1834. Gallica-Centifolia hybrid. Medium, double, light vivid pink. Not the same as 'Irena'.

Iris Nova. Pink shaded white.

Isabella [#1] ('Prolifère'). Before 1834. Full, rich rose color.

Isabella [#2]. Before 1838. Medium, very full, compact, velvety crimson, shaded and streaked with purple. Upright growth.

Isabelle. See 'Grande Agathe Nouvelle'.

Isabelle de Lorraine. Vibert, France, 1843. Very large, double, rose-pink, spotted. Paler at circumference. Compact, branching growth.

Iseult. 1846. Gallica-China hybrid. Large, double, very bright rose-pink. Isolde of medieval tales.

Isoline. Before 1848. Large, double, rose-pink, edged lilac. Vigorous, upright growth.

Jacques Dessailles. Flesh pink blooms.

James Mason   **70**

Jane Seymour. Before 1848. Large, double, compact, well-formed, pale lilac-pink with a deeper rose-colored center. Vigorous, upright growth. Not the same as below-listed 'Jeanne Seymour'. Third wife of Henry VIII.

Janus. Before 1934. Roman deity of entrances; most ancient king of Italy.

Jaqueline. Before 1834.

Jason. Miellez, France. Pink. Greek hero.

Jean. Crimson.

Jean Bart [#1]. Trébucien, France, before 1838. Very large, double, velvety dark vivid crimson.

Jean Bart [#2]. Vibert, France, 1841. Medium, double, rose-pink, spotted.

Jeanne d'Albret. Vibert, France, 1819. Large, very full, pink bloom, shaded with paler border. (Possibly originally from van Eeden, or earlier.)

Jeanne de Lavel. 1834. Large, double, cupped, bright rose color, occasionally spotted.

Jeanne d'Urfe [#1]. Vibert, France. Lilac crimson.

Jeanne d'Urfe [#2]. 1841. Gallica-Centifolia hybrid. Very large, double, cupped, mauve-rose with a blush circumference. Vigorous, branching growth.

Jeanne Gray. See 'Agathe Ombrée'.

Jeanne Hachette   71

Jeanne Mailotte. Miellez, France. Lilac.

Jeanne Seymour. Pale pink flowers.

Jeannette   71

Jeanne Vertpert. Before 1834. Carmine shaded. Large, very full, and compact.

Jean Sellier. Lilac pink.

Jefferson. Descemet, France. Deep crimson.

Je Me Maintiendrai. France, before 1846. Gallica-China hybrid. Large, very double, expanded blooms. Rose-pink. Vigorous, branching growth.

Jennelon. Miellez, France. Lilac.

Jenny. See 'Jenny Duval'.

Jenny Delacharme. Hardy, France, 1827. Medium, very full, well-formed, flattened pink blossoms in clusters. Growth wider than tall.

Jenny Duval   **70**, 71

Jeune Henri. Before 1813. In Joséphine's collection.

Jezabel. Pean, France, 1826. Medium, very full, vivid purple-crimson.

Jolie Parmentier. Crimson violet.

Josephina   71

Joséphine [#1] ('L'Aimable Beauté de Stors', 'Ninon de l'Enclos'). Vibert, France, 1817. Large, double, deep pink blossoms, paler at edges.

Joséphine [#2]. Boutigny, France, before 1838. Medium, semi-double, bright crimson, spotted.

Joséphine Fouquier. Lilac-purple blossoms.

Joséphine Maille. Boutigny, France, before 1838. Large, double, vivid pink.

Joséphine Oudin. Before 1848. Gallica-Centifolia hybrid. Medium, very full, cupped, creamy white. Upright growth.

Joséphine Parmentier   71

Joseph Wattecamps. Pink.

Juanita   71

Julianna. Before 1848. An all but unknown pink Gallica.

Julie d'Estanges   71

Julie Everaertz. Deep bright crimson.

Juliette   **72**, 73

Juno   73

Junon. See 'Belle Junon' [#1].

Junon à Fleurs Pleines. Prévost, France. Deep pink.

Justine. See 'La Triomphante' [#2].

Karaiskaki. Prévost, France, before 1838. Mid-size, double, convex, crimson-purple to dark purple with paler edges.

Kean [#1]   73

Kean [#2]. Date and origin unknown. Clear pink.

Keller. Deep pink blossoms.

Kellner. Pink.

King of Rome ('Ponceau Parfait', 'Theodore de Corse'). Before 1844. Double, compact, ranunculus-form. Well-shaped, bright crimson. Not the same as 'Roi de Rome'.

King of Roses. See 'Roi des Roses'.

Klèber. See 'Général Klèber'.

Königin. Before 1834.

Kreinii. Wine and violet.

Kretly. Bardon, 1842. Medium, double, violet, spotted with purple.

Krey. Germany. Carmine and violet.

Labby de Pompières. Prévost, France, 1827. Large, double, convex, bright evenly colored pink. Fragrant.

La Béguine. Before 1848. Gallica-China hybrid. Large, double, crimson, spotted and shaded cream.

La Belle Africaine. See 'Africaine'.

La Belle Elize. Before 1846. Large, well-formed, blush.

La Belle Mariée. Before 1846. Very double, crimson.

La Belle Sultane   16, 73, **75**

La Belle Violette. See 'Belle Violette'.

Laborde (de Laborde). Violet-purple.

La Bordée de Rouge. White and pink.

La Calaisienne. Vibert, France, before 1848. Gallica-Centifolia hybrid. Large, double, compact, well-formed, pink. Vigorous, upright growth.

La Capricieuse. Before 1846. Mid-size, full, bright rose, pencil-thin streaks of white.

La Changeante. See 'Changeante'.

La Chéri. Before 1834.

La Chiffonée. Before 1834.

La Circassienne. Vibert, France, 1821. Large, double, light but bright pink, evenly colored. Blooms in clusters.

La Cocarde. See 'La Majestueuse' [#1].

La Comtesse ('La Terminale'). Vibert or possibly Prévost, France, 1819. Medium, very double, convex, light crimson-purple.

La Constance. 1817. Clear pink bordered flesh pink.

La Coquette. See 'Belle de Cels'.

La Couronne de Roses. Deep pink blossoms.

La Couronne du Président. Crimson, spotted.

La Couronne Pourpre. Before 1834.

La Couronne Tendre. Velvety purple.

La Covenable. Before 1838. Medium, full, rich lilac-pink.

La Délicieuse. Before 1838. Medium to large, uniformly colored pale pink. Profuse bloom. Vigorous growth with glaucous foliage. Possibly a Gallica-Centifolia hybrid by Vibert.

La Désirée. Descemet, France, before 1834.

L'Admirable. Before 1813. Gallica-Centifolia hybrid. Mid-size, full flesh pink.

La Dominante. Miellez, France, before 1838. Large, full, well-formed, pale pink, reflexing petals.

La Duchesse. Before 1838. Gallica-Centifolia hybrid. Large, very full, bright rose-pink.

Lady Cooper. Before 1848. Gallica-China hybrid. Large, double, cupped blossoms of bright rose-pink.

Lady Fitzgerald. Noisette, France, 1827. Possibly an Agathe rose. Large, very full, white blooms with a pale blush in clusters.

Lady Fitzharris. Laffay, France, before 1848. Gallica-China hybrid. Large, double, pale lilac, veined and marbled light rose.

Lady Hamilton. Before 1834. Gallica-China hybrid. Large, double, compact, crimson blooms, shaded purple. Mistress of Admiral Nelson.

Lady Jeanne Grey. See 'Agathe Ombrée'.

Lady Macbeth. Parmentier, Belgium. Deep pink.

Lady Morgan. Girardon, France, before 1838. Large, very double, well-formed, bright pink blooms in clusters. Vigorous, branching growth.

Lady Peel. See 'Duc d'Angoulême' [#1].

Lady Stuart ('Leipodicella'). Before 1848. Gallica-China hybrid. Large, double, cupped, silvery blush-pink.

Lady Tankerville. See 'Britannicus'.

Lady Thenermill. See 'Britannicus'.

Laetitia ('La Volupté', 'Letitia'). Before 1848. Gallica-Centifolia hybrid. Large, full, cupped, well-formed, lilac-rose blooms, veined.

La Favorite. Descemet, France, before 1844. Bright cherry-crimson.

Lafayette. See 'Général Lafayette'.

La Fidèle ('Fidèle'). Miellez, France, before 1838. Gallica-Centifolia hybrid. Very large, full, lilac-rose.

La Fille de l'Air. 1845. Gallica-Centifolia hybrid. Large, double pale flesh pink.

La Flamboyante. Godefroy, France. Bluish purple.

La Fontaine [#1]. Before 1848. Very large, full, globular. Lilac-crimson. French writer of fables.

La Fontaine [#2]. Vibert, France, 1846. Gallica-China hybrid. Medium, double, purple.

La Géorgienne. Laffay, France, before 1838. Gallica-Centifolia hybrid. Mid-size full blooms. Pink with paler border.

La Glacée ('La Gloire', 'La Victorie', 'Uniflore'). Before 1838. Medium, double, pale lilac.

La Globuleuse. Before 1846. Large, very full, very globular, dull purple-crimson. Upright growth.

La Gloire. See 'La Glacée'.

La Gloire des Agathes. Before 1834.

La Glorieuse [#1] ('La Gracieuse', 'Belle de Hesse', 'Singleton', 'La Prédestinée' [#1], 'Illustre', 'La Triomphante' [#1], 'Rex Nigrorum', 'Surpasse Singleton', 'Subrotundifolia crenata'). Godefroy, France, before 1813. Medium, full, lilac-rose, shaded light purple. In Joséphine's collection.

La Glorieuse [#2]. Calvert, France, before 1838. Small, very double, convex, rich velvety violet-purple.

La Gracieuse. See 'La Glorieuse' [#1].

La Grande Belle Pourpre. Before 1834.

La Grandeur ('Grandeur'). Laffay, France, before 1834. Gallica-China hybrid. Large, double, compact, dark rose-pink.

L'Aimable Beauté. See 'Nouveau Triomphe'.

L'Aimable Beauté de Stors. See 'Joséphine' [#1].

La Jeune Reine. Before 1848. Double, cupped, vivid rose.

La Juive. Lilac-purple flowers.

La Julie. Descemet, France.

La Louise   74

La Maculée 74

La Magnifique. See 'Pourpre Charmant'.

La Majestueuse [#1] ('La Cocarde', 'Lucrece'). Medium, full, convex, vivid pink, paler edge.

La Majestueuse [#2]. ('Perle de l'Orient', 'Carmin Lisere', 'La Moskowa'. Godefroy, France, 1817. Semi-double, reddish purple with violet circumference.

L'Ambassadeur. Miellez, France. Crimson shaded.

L'Ambre Pourpre. Before 1834.

La Mère Gigogne. Descemet, France.

La Merveille. Descemet, France.

L'Ami Déscartes. Before 1848. Gallica-China hybrid. Large purple-crimson blooms.

La Mignonne. Before 1834. Possibly a Centifolia.

La Mignonne de Fleurs. Before 1834.

La Moskowa. See 'La Majestueuse' [#2].

L'Amoureuse. See 'Andromaque' [#1].

La Napolitaine. See 'Bandeau de Soliman'.

La Nationale 76

La Négresse. See 'Perle von Weissenstein'.

La Neige 76

La Nina. Descemet, France.

La Noble Fleur ('Leander', 'Pelletier's Rose'). Pelletier, France, before 1838. Medium, full, evenly colored soft pink. Profuse early bloom.

La Nubienne. See 'Gloire des Héllènes'.

Laodicée. Sommerson, 1823. Very large, full, well-formed blooms. Blush, spotted rose-pink. Fair maid of Homeric legend.

Laomédon. Miellez, France, before 1838. Large, double, lilac-pink with a very pale circumference. King of Troy; father of Priam.

La Parfaite Double. Before 1834.

La Parisienne. Hardy, France, before 1834. Light crimson. Possibly a Damask.

La Pintad ('Pintade'). Before 1813. In Joséphine's collection at Malmaison. Pink, spotted white.

La Planette. Before 1834.

La Plus Belle des Panachée. Pink shaded and striped.

La Plus Belle des Ponctuées 76

La Plus Belle des Violettes ('Gloria Mundi'). Calvert, France, before 1834. Small, very double, purple, marbled or shaded with violet.

La Plus Rouge. Before 1834. Crimson.

La Porte. Parmentier, Belgium. Deep pink.

La Possédée. Purple blooms.

La Précieuse ('Précieuse' [#1]). Hardy, France, before 1813. Gallica-Centifolia hybrid. Very full, well-formed, pink to pale-pink blooms. Petals on circumference crinkled in center, rolled in a ring. Blossoms in clusters. In Joséphine's collection.

La Prédestinée [#1]. See 'La Glorieuse' [#1].

La Prédestinée [#2] ('Queen of Nigritia, 'Regina Nigrorum' 'Reine de Nigritia'). Godefroy, France, 1823. Medium, loosely double, dark bluish purple, shaded black and violet.

La Princesse. Prévost, France, before 1838. Medium, full, vivid deep rose to light crimson.

La Princesse des Galles. Before 1834. Agathe rose.

La Pucelle ('Théagène'). Vibert, France, 1820. Large, very double, lilac with a rose-colored center and paler border. Branching growth.

La Pyramidale. See 'Belle de Cels'.

La Quarantième. Before 1848. Gallica-China hybrid. Lilac-rose.

Laquemont. See 'Alexandre Laquement'.

La Ravissante. Before 1838. Agathe rose. Medium, very full, pink.

L'Archevêque. Purple, shaded violet.

La Reine d'Amateur ('La Reine des Amateurs'). Mme. Hébert, France, before 1834. Lilac with a paler border.

La Reine de Russe. Before 1834.

La Reine des Amateurs. See 'La Reine d'Amateur'.

La Reine des Roses ('Reine des Roses' 'Queen of Roses' 'Black Ranunculus Rose of Holland'). Paillard, Holland, before 1834. Small, doubled, velvety dark purple, shaded blackish-purple.

La Renomée. Before 1834. Perhaps yet another name for 'Belle de Cels'!

Large Clustering Provins. Joly, France, before 1838.

La Rochefoucauld. Coquerel, France, 1825. Clear pink, shaded. French author and moralist.

La Rochefoucauld Liancourt [#1]. France, before 1838. Very large, double, convex. A vivid rose color in center, blush streaked light purple at edges.

La Rochefoucauld Liancourt [#2]. Vibert, France, before 1838. Gallica-China hybrid. Globular, vivid crimson blooms in clusters.

La Roxelane 76

La Rubanée [#1]. See 'Gallique Panachée'.

La Rubanée [#2]. See 'Village Maid'.

Las-Casas d'Angers ('Las-Cases'). Vibert, France, 1828. Large, full, cupped, carmine blooms, marbled and shaded purple-crimson. Tall. Named for de Las-Cases, historian and friend of Napoléon.

La Somptueuse. See 'Clémentine Joineaux'.

La Splendeur ('La Splendor'). Before 1846. Medium, double, compact, vivid crimson to dark purple, mottled white. Small upright growth.

Lasthenie. Before 1848. Gallica-China hybrid. Mid-sized, doubled, cupped, rose-lilac, shaded lilac.

La Superbe. See 'Couronne Impériale'.

La Suprise. Before 1834.

La Sylphide. Before 1848. Mid-size, full, cupped, blush-rose, petals edged with white. Branching growth.

La Tendresse 76

La Tenterelle ('Belle de Parny', 'Parny'). Laffay, France, before 1826. Gallica-China hybrid. Large, full, cupped, rose color, shaded mauve and slate.

La Terminale. See 'La Comtesse'.

Latone. Laffay, France, before 1848. Very large, full, cupped, rose-pink, mottled with mauve-gray. Vigorous, upright growth.

La Tour d'Auvergne. Vibert, France, 1842. Gallica-Centifolia hybrid. Large, double, cupped, rich rose-crimson, tinged purple. Brighter center. Upright growth.

La Très Sombre. 1820. Blackish purple blooms.

La Triomphante [#1]. See 'La Glorieuse' [#1].

La Triomphante [#2] ('Nouvelle de Province', 'Justine' 'Rosa Pyramidata'). Vibert, France, 1822. Pale pink.

La Triomphe. See 'Aimable Rouge'.

L'Attrayante. Laffay, France, 1847. Gallica-China hybrid. Mid-size, full ranunculus-form, flesh pink.

Laure Audenet. Godefroy, France. Pale pink with a more deeply colored center.

Lavalette. Prévost, France, before 1838. Mid-size, very full, lilac-pink.

La Vallière ('Vallière'). Vibert, France, 1846. Gallica-Centifolia hybrid. Large, double, flesh pink. Comtesse de La Vallière, mistress of Louis XIV.

La Venue. Before 1848. Large, double, compact, crimson to purple.

La Vestale. Robert, France, before 1848. Gallica-Centifolia hybrid. Medium, full, cupped, creamy white. Upright growth.

La Veuve [#1] ('Le Deuil', 'The Widow Rose'). Prévost, France, before 1838. Medium, very full, extremely dark violet-purple, streaked and edged paler.

La Veuve [#2] ('Aigle de Prusse'). Lilac-crimson with a paler border.

La Victoire. See 'La Glacée'.

La Victorieuse. Before 1834.

La Villageoise. See 'Gallique Panachée'.

La Ville de Grand. Robert, France, before 1848. Large, double, expanded, bright pink, edged with blush-lavender. Small, pendulous growth.

La Ville de Londres. See 'Ville de Londres'.

Lavinie. Pale pink. Queen of Latium and second wife of Aeneas.

Lavoisier [#1]. Lacompte, France, before 1838. Mid-size, double, light purple-crimson. Nearly thornless. Named after the French chemist.

Lavoisier [#2]. 1842. Mid-size, full, well-formed, compact blooms. Rich lilac-rose, finely spotted with white. Variegated foliage.

La Volupté. See 'Laetitia'.

Léa. Vétillard, France. Deep crimson.

Leander. See 'La Noble Fleur'. From a Greek myth, lover of the priestess Hero.

Le Baron Louis. See 'Baron Louis'.

Le Beau Mulâtre. Before 1834.

L'Éblouissante de la Queue. Noisette, France, before 1848. Dark velvety crimson, large, very full blooms with a brighter center. Compact upright growth.

Le Cafre. Purple, spotted blossoms.

Le Cordon Bleu. See 'Cordon Bleu'.

Leda. Before 1834. From Greek mythology, the mother of Castor, Pollux, Helen, and Clytemnestra.

Le Deuil. See 'La Veuve' [#1].

Le Diable Boiteux. Before 1848. Large, double, clear rose and white.

Ledonneau-Leblanc   76

Lee [#1]. ('Ex Albo Rosea' 'Belle Aurore'). Vibert, France, 1823. Large, very full, expanded, blush-pink, shaded flesh. Profuse, early bloom.

Lee [#2] ('The Lee Rose'). Before 1838. Large, double, bright rose-pink. Branching growth.

Lee's Carnation. Double, cupped, crimson blossoms, striped with pink.

Le Flavia Bleuâtre. Before 1846. Bluish lilac, marbled.

Le Grand Couronne Cramoisie. Before 1834.

Le Grand Mogul. See 'Grand Mogul'.

Le Grand Palais. 1824. Gallica-Centifolia hybrid. Very large, pink.

Le Grand Sultan. See 'Grande Sultane' [#1].

Le Grand Triomphe ('Le Triomphe', 'Pavot' [#3], 'Grand Pivoine de Lille'). Miellez, France, before 1838. Gallica-Centifolia hybrid. Well-formed blossoms, light purple, tinged mauve-gray.

Le Grand Visir. Before 1834.

Leipodicella. See 'Lady Stuart'.

Le Jacobin. See 'Marcel Bourgoin'.

L'Élégante [#1]. See 'Euphrosyne L'Élégante'.

L'Élégante [#2]. Before 1838. Agathe rose. Large, very full, pale pink. Vigorous growth.

Lemarque. See 'Général Lemarque'.

Le Maure de Venise. See 'Othello' [#2].

L'Empereur. Before 1813. In Joséphine's collection at Malmaison. Named by Joséphine for Napoléon.

L'Enchantée. Miellez, France. Flesh pink.

L'Enchanteresse   77

L'Enfant de France. See 'Enfant de France' [#1].

Lenfroy. Joly, France, 1836.

Lénore d'Este. Vétillard, France. Marbled blossoms.

Léocadie. Hardy, France, before 1838. Gallica-Centifolia hybrid. Large, very full, flesh pink.

Léonard de Vinci. Robert and Moreau, France, 1861. Deep pink.

Leonea. Before 1848. Large, double, cupped, vivid rose color.

Leonel Dumoustier. Before 1848. Double, cupped, light rose-pink.

Léonidas. Sommesson, before 1838. Large, double, bright rose-pink. Peony-form blossom. Spartan king.

Léonide. Clear purple flowers.

Léontine. Vibert, France, 1820. Large, double, pink with a paler circumference.

Léon X. Before 1846. Very large, double, well-formed, compact, rose-pink blooms with a circumference of lavender-blush. Vigorous, branching growth.

Léopard Rose. Before 1846.

Leopold. Before 1846. Medium, double, dark crimson, shaded black.

Le Pérou. Prévost, France. Purple.

Le Phoenix   77

Le Prince. ('The Prince', 'Le Prince Régent'). Before 1846. Bright crimson spotted blush.

Le Prince de Chimay. Parmentier, Belgium. Flesh pink.

Le Rosier Évêque. See 'The Bishop'.

Lesbos. Before 1834.

Les Mages. See 'Gentil'.

Le Soleil. Crimson blooms.

Le Solitaire. Flesh pink.

Lesponda. See 'Bandeau de Soliman'.

L'Esponia. See 'Bandeau de Soliman'.

Les Saisons d'Italie   77

Les Trois Mages. See 'Gentil'.

Le Styx. Parmentier, Belgium. Deep purple.

Le Tasse. Parmentier, Belgium. Purple.

Letitia. See 'Laetitia'.

Le Triomphe. See 'Le Grand Triomphe'.

L'Évêque. See 'The Bishop'.

Lévêque. Violet, spotted. Different from above.

Leyden. Before 1834. A Dutch painter.

Le 29 Julliet. See 'Cocinea Superba'.

L'Hospital. See 'Hospitalière'.

L'Hospitalière. See 'Hospitalière'.

Lie de Vin Double. Descemet, France.

L'Impératrice Joséphine. See 'Empress Joséphine'.

Lincelle ('Rose Lincelle'). Before 1838. Medium, very full, clear violet with a crimson-violet edge.

L'Incomparable de Lille. See 'Incomparable de Lille'.

L'Ingénue   77

L'Intéressante. See 'Intéressante'.

Lionel de Moutiers. Pale pink.

Lisbeth. Before 1848. Gallica-Centifolia hybrid. Medium, double, cupped, delicate blush-pink. Branching growth.

Lively. Before 1834.

L'Obsurité. Prévost, France, before 1834. Medium, semi-double, violet, shaded purple.

Loisel. Prévost, France, before 1826. Large, double, deep crimson with paler edges.

L'Ombre Panachée. See 'Ombre Panachée'.

L'Ombre Superbe. Before 1834.

London Bridge. Before 1834.

Lord Byron. Before 1834. Mid-size, very full, cupped, lilac blooms, mottled purple and blush. Compact, upright growth.

Lord Keith. Before 1848. Gallica-China hybrid. Large, double, cupped, rich rose color, marbled mauve.

Lord Londonderry. Crimson.

Lord Nelson. Before 1848. Gallica-China hybrid. Mid-size, double, cupped, dark velvety crimson-purple. A British admiral and author of one of my favorite quotes: "Men and ships rot in port."

Lord Strangfort. Before 1834.

Lord Wellington ('Wellington'). Vibert, France, before 1838. Medium, double, cupped, crimson-purple.

L'Orientale. Couquerel, France, before 1838. Medium, very double, vivid purple-crimson with paler edges.

Louis Carlier. Wine crimson.

Louise Méhul. Parmentier, Belgium, before 1834. Large, flattened, light crimson, spotted white.

Louis Foucquier. Before 1848. Large, expanded dark crimson.

Louis Fries. Before 1848. Gallica-China hybrid. Large, full, globular blush-pink.

Louis Lecker. Before 1848. Large, double, cupped, blush. Branching, upright growth.

Louis Le Grand. Miellez, France. Crimson.

Louis Leneveu. Joly, France, 1836. Carmine.

Louis Parmentier. Parmentier, Belgium. Pink.

Louis Philippe [#1]   77

Louis Phillipe [#2]. Guerin, France, 1834. Gallica-China hybrid. Large, very doubled and cupped, purplish mid-pink with a paler circumference. Vigorous branching growth and spicy fragrance.

Louis van Till. See 'Louis van Tyle'.

Louis van Tyle   77

Louis van Tyll. See 'Louis van Tyle'.

Louis XII. Coquerel, France, before 1838. Medium, full, expanded, light bright lilac-pink.

Louis XIV [#1]. Hardy, France, 1824. Large, double, clear light pink.

Louis XIV [#2]. Before 1838. Large, very full, well-formed, clear vivid pink.

Louis XVI de Lyon. Before 1834.

Louis XVIII [#1]. See 'Gallica Maxima Gigantea'.

Louis XVIII [#2] ('Louis XVIII Nouveau'). France, 1826. Large, very full, bluish violet.

Lubée. Before 1834.

Lucca. Before 1834.

Lucile Dubourg. Dubourg, France, 1826. Velvety.

Lucille. Before 1846. Clear pink, spotted white.

Lucille Duplessis   77

Lucrèce. See 'La Majestueuse' [#1].

Ludvicus. Calvert, France, before 1838. Medium, full dark bluish violet.

Luride. Before 1834.

Lustré d'Église   78

Lydia de Forbin. Noisette. France, 1827. Crimson.

Lyre de Flore. See 'Phénix'.

Maculé de Montmorency. Before 1848. Medium, full, expanded rosy-purple, sometimes edged and spotted white. Upright growth.

Mme. Audiot. Before 1848. Very large, double, compact, lilac with a rose-pink center.

Mme. Audot. Verdier, France, 1844. Gallica-Alba hybrid. Large, doubled, cupped, cream, tinged blush with a deeper blush center.

Mme. Boursault. See 'Agathe Boursault'.

Mme. Campan. Before 1848. Medium, full, cupped, bright rose-pink, mottled mauve.

Mme. Christophe ('Reine des Nègres', 'Nigritiana' [#2], 'Nigritienne'). Calvert (or Coquerel), France, before 1834. Small, double, very dark velvety purple with brown tones.

Mme. Cottin ('Sophie Cottin'). Before 1846. Very large,

doubled, expanded, deep pink. Vigorous, upright growth.

Mme. Dacier. Carmine.

Mme. Damoureau. Large, very full, compact, deep crimson-rose.

Mme. de Coster. Deep pink flowers.

Mme. Deshoulières. See 'Deshoulières'.

Mme. Desmoutiers. Clear purple-crimson.

Mme. de St. Hermine. Before 1848. Gallica-China hybrid. Rosy pink.

Mme. d'Hébray   78

Mme. Domoraan. Deep pink.

Mme. Dubarry. Before 1846. Mid-size, full, expanded, vivid crimson, shaded dark crimson. Vigorous, branching growth.

Mme. Fontaine. Salmon pink.

Mme. Hébert. See 'Président de Sèze'.

Mme. Henriette. Before 1848. Gallica-Centifolia hybrid. Large, doubled, cupped, well-formed, lilac-rose with blush circumference.

Mme. Huet. Before 1848. Gallica-Centifolia hybrid. Mid-size, full pale flesh with a blush circumference and mottled white.

Mme. Hurette. Deep pink blooms.

Mme. L'Abbey. Before 1848. Gallica-Centifolia hybrid. Large, full, cupped, vivid rose-pink.

Mme. Oudinot. Dark clear pink.

Mme. Pisaroni. Before 1848. Gallica-China hybrid. Large, cupped, vivid rose-pink.

Mme. Poncey ('Poncey'). Before 1848. Gallica-China hybrid. Crimson-purple.

Mme. Quételet. Parmentier, Belgium, 1830. Pink, shaded.

Mme. Rameau. Before 1848. Gallica-China hybrid. Large, double, rich dark, velvety purple.

Madame Roland [#1]. See 'Couronne Royale'.

Mme. Roland [#2]. Girardon, France, before 1838. Gallica-Centifolia hybrid. Double, fragrant, pale pink.

Mme. Sandeur. Before 1848. Gallica-Centifolia hybrid. Medium, full, delicate flesh pink.

Mme. Saportas. Large, double, vivid rose-pink. Very fragrant.

Mme. Sommesson. Pale pink flowers.

Mme. Ville 78

Madelon Frequet. See 'Madelon Friquet'.

Madelon Friquet 78

Mademoiselle. Vibert, France. Flesh pink, paler edge.

Mlle. Boursault. Noisette, France, before 1838. Agathe rose. Medium, very full, fringed petals, white tinged with blush.

Mlle. de la Serna. Parmentier, Belgium. Pale pink.

Mlle. Duchesnois. Before 1848. Large, very full, cupped, blush or flesh pink with a pale rose center.

Mlle. Laffay. Before 1838. Medium, double, flesh pink, edged white.

Mlle. Montessu. Before 1848. Flesh pink.

Mlle. Sontag. Rich pink with pale blush reverse on petals.

Magdalen. Before 1834.

Magna Flore Belle. Before 1834.

Magna Rosea. Before 1848. Gallica-China hybrid. Very large, very double, cupped, pale rose-pink.

Magnifique ('Magnifique à Fleurs Cerise'). Prévost, France, before 1838. Very large, semi-double blossoms of vivid cherry-purple.

Maheca Nova ('Maheka Nova', 'Nouveau Maheca'). Godefroy, France, 1818. Dark, semi-double, velvety brownish purple blooms. It is entirely possible that 'Maheka Nova' is the same rose as 'Nouvelle Maheca'; if so, all the synonyms for both may be later names given to 'Passe Velours'. Descemet had left Paris by 1818; perhaps when Godefroy added this very distinctive rose to his lists he took the liberty of renaming it.

Maheka. van Eeden, Holland, before 1834.

Mahl ('Mohl'). Before 1848. Large, very full, cupped, deep carmine.

Maître d'École. See 'Rose du Maître d'École'.

Majestueuse 78

Malek Adel ('Melik el Adel'). Before 1848. Large, very double, mauve pink, spotted white.

Malesherbes 78

Malherb. Circa 1848. Very large, double, bright purple with a vivid crimson center. Branching growth.

Malinoise. Deep pink blossoms.

Mallow Rose. See 'Mauve'.

Malton 78

Malvina. Hardy, France, before 1838. Large, very full, well-formed, cupped, ashen-pink, paling to white at the circumference. Profuse flowering. Blossoms in clusters. Vigorous growth.

Manette. Before 1838. Medium, full, evenly colored rich crimson-rose with pale circumference.

Manon. Miellez, France. Lilac-pink.

Manteau d'Évêque. Violet, spotted white.

Manteau Impérial. See 'Britannicus'.

Manteau Pourpre 78

Manteau Royal 79

Mapivoine du Roi. Deep pink.

Marceau [#1]. Before 1834.

Marceau [#2]. Vibert, France, 1844. Medium, double, rich rose color, spotted with pale rose.

Marcel Bourgoin 79

Maréchal Bertrand. Before 1834.

Maréchal d'Ancre. Parmentier, Belgium. Pink.

Maréchal de Tavannes. Parmentier, Belgium. Deep wine crimson.

Maréchal Lannes. Before 1848. Gallica-China hybrid. Medium, double, compact, bright cherry crimson.

Maréchal Mortier. See 'Deuil de Maréchal Mortier'.

Maréchal Soult. Laffay, France, 1838. Gallica-China hybrid. Medium, full, cupped, light vermilion.

Margaretha. Before 1834.

Margaret Mary. Before 1848. Large, very full, cupped, purplish rose with a deeper rose center.

Marquerite. Hardy, France, 1827. Purple, striped white.

Marguerite de Valois [#1]. Before 1834. Very large, double, compact, rose-pink. Branching growth. French queen.

Marguerite de Valois [#2]. Vibert, France, 1843. Gallica hybrid. Large, double, crimson.

Marguerite Lancezeur. Before 1848. Large, double, lilac-crimson with pale edges. Upright growth.

Marie. Noisette, France, before 1848. Gallica-China hybrid. Large, full, cupped, vivid violet-pink.

Marie Antoinette 79

Marie de Burgogne. Vibert, France, before 1848. Gallica-hybrid. Very large, double, rose-pink, spotted white.

Marie de Champlouis. Before 1848. Gallica-China hybrid.

Large, full, cupped, rich crimson with the circumference marbled mauve-gray.

Marie des Moutiers. Circa 1900. Clear rose.

Marie Fouquier. Dark crimson blooms.

Marie Joséphine. Prévost, France, 1828. Medium, double, even flesh pink. Profuse bloom.

Marie Louise. See 'A Fleurs Gigantesques'.

Marie Prévost. Before 1848. Gallica-China hybrid. Cupped, blush pink with a rich crimson center.

Marie Stuart ('Mary Stuart'). Prévost, France, before 1818. Medium, full, light purple, spotted at the circumference. Blooms profusely in clusters.

Marie Thérèse. Robert and Moreau, France, 1838. Salmon pink.

Marie Tudor 79

Marie Van Baerle. Germany. Pink.

Marinette. Vibert, France, 1819. Possibly a Gallica-Centifolia hybrid. Large, double, flesh pink.

Marion. Agathe rose. Before 1838. Medium, pale lilac-pink.

Mariquita. Before 1848. Large, double, lilac-rose.

Maritorne. Robert, France, 1831. Large, double, flesh pink. Sometimes classified as a Portland.

Marjolin ('Rose Marjolin'). Roeser, France. Very large, double, well-formed, violet-crimson blooms.

Marmorea Belgica. Dark lilac. Marbled.

Marmorea Plena. Before 1834. Marbled.

Marquis de Dreux Brézé. Crimson and clear pale pink.

Marquis de la Romana. Prévost, France, before 1834. Small to medium, double, pink.

Marquis de Monterat. Flesh pink.

Marquis de Trazegnies. Deep pink blossoms.

Marquise d'Alpré. Before 1848. Gallica-Centifolia hybrid. Large, double, clear lilac rose.

Marquise d'Exéter. Paul, England. Salmon pink.

Marquis of Lothian. Before 1848. Mid-size, full, expanded, peach-pink with a blush circumference. Profuse bloom and branching growth.

Mary Stuart. See 'Marie Stuart'.

Mathilde de Mondeville. Before 1848. Gallica-Centifolia hybrid. Medium, double, globular, blush, shaded pale flesh pink. Pendulous growth and profuse bloom.

Matilda. Before 1844. Handsome, very doubled. Clear pink.

Matthieu Molé. Vibert, France, before 1848. Medium, double, compact, well-formed, rose-crimson, mottled purple. Upright growth.

Maubach. Vibert, France, before 1848. Gallica-China hybrid. Mid-size, double, blackish purple.

Mauget. Before 1838. Small, very double, convex purple with a paler circumference. Possibly a Gallica-Centifolia hybrid.

Maupertuis. Robert and Moreau, France.

Maure de virginée. van Eeden, Holland, before 1834.

Mauve ('Rose Mauve', 'Rose Visqueuse', 'Pavot' [#2], *Rosa Inermis sub-albo Violacea*). Vibert, France, before 1838. Medium, semi-double, lilac-crimson blooms, streaked bluish lilac. Thornless. Latin name from Gore, interesting as *R. inermis* Thory is *R. x francofurtana*. "Mallow Rose" is English translation for *mauve*. A sticky mess, indeed.

Max d'Aremberg. Pale pink.

Maxima. See 'Sultana'.

Maxime ('Maximum'). Noisette, France, 1827. Purple.

Maximus. See 'Clara'.

Mazeppa 79

Mazzeppa. See 'Mazeppa'. 79

Mécène 79

Medée. Before 1848. Cupped, blush with a deeper pink center.

Méhul ('Rose Méhul'). Cartier, France, 1826. Large, full blooms of violet-carmine. A French composer (1763-1817).

Mélange de Beautés. Miellez, France. Crimson.

Melanie. Vibert, France, before 1848. Gallica-China hybrid. Large, full, compact, well-formed blossoms of a bright rose color. Upright growth.

Melanie Waldor. Vibert, France, before 1838. Gallica-Centifolia hybrid. Medium, double, cupped, chalky white. Upright growth.

Melpomène. Parmentier, Belgium. Pink. Muse of tragedy.

Mélusine. Before 1848. Medium, full, mauve-violet. Fairy of a French fable who was transformed into a half-serpentine being.

Mercedes 79

Mère Brune. Miellez, France. Purple.

Mère Gigone. Before 1838. Medium, full, vivid light pink.

Merveille de l'Univers. Belgium, before 1838. Large, very full, carmine with a lilac circumference.

Merveille du Monde. Deep pink.

Merveilleuse Beauté. Miellez, France. Pink.

Merveilleuse de Noisette. Noisette, France. Purple with violet shadings.

Mervillon. Before 1834.

Meunière. Parmentier, Belgium. Deep purple-crimson.

Meunière de Santis. Pink.

Meuricie. Before 1848. Large, double, globular rose-pink.

Mexicana Aurantica. See 'Tricolore' [#1].

Mexicana Bolivar. Before 1834.

Mexicana Violacea. Before 1834.

Meyerbeer. Carmine. Opera composer (1791-1864).

Miceala [#1]. Vibert, France. Cerise.

Micaela [#2]. Moreau and Robert, France, 1864. Gallica-Centifolia hybrid. Medium, very full, compact, blush, shaded deeper pink. Upright growth, profuse bloom.

Michel-Ange. Verdier, France, 1847. Pink. [Michelangelo].

Mine d'Or. See 'Bouquet Pourpre'.

Minerve. Before 1813. In Joséphine's collection. Deep crimson. Roman goddess of wisdom, Athena.

Minette. Before 1848. Gallica-China hybrid. Mid-size, double, globular, peach-pink.

Minos. Robert, France, before 1846. Large, very full, compact, bright rose, spotted flesh pink. Legendary king of Crete.

Mirabelle. Before 1834.

Miralba. Before 1848. Gallica-China hybrid. Small, double, compact, blackish crimson-purple.

Miranda. Parmentier, Belgium. Purple flowers.

Miss Wright. Vibert, France, 1825.

Mrs. Rivers. Before 1848. Gallica-Centifolia hybrid. Large, double, cupped, rich blush-pink with a nearly white circumference.

Mithridates. Hardy, France, 1824. Large, full, well-formed, vivid crimson. King of Pontus, ancient kingdom in Asia Minor on Black Sea.

Modeste Guerin. Guerin, France, 1833. Gallica hybrid. Mid-size, double, cupped, rose-pink, mottled and splashed white.

Mogul. Before 1834.

Mohl. See 'Mahl'.

Moïse [#1] 79

Moïse [#2]. Miellez, France. Cerise.

Mollevaut. Noisette, France, 1827. Crimson.

Mon Ami Jérôme. Parmentier, Belgium.

Monarchie. Carmine blossoms.

Mon Bijou. Before 1834.

Mon Caprice. Miellez, France. Crimson.

Mon Hortense. Vétillard, France, 1827. Pink, spotted.

Monime. Vibert, France, 1840. Medium, full rich crimson-rose, spotted light purple.

Monplaisir. Calvert, France. Purple.

Monsieur. See 'Cramoisi des Alpes'.

Monsieur Henschier. Germany. Purple.

Monsieur Krey. Germany. Carmine and violet.

Monsieur Richter. Germany. Carmine-purple.

Monstrosa. Before 1834. If this rose was the same as 'Montruosa', a Centifolia, then probably with few Gallica traits.

Montalembert 80

Montault. See 'Évêque d'Angers'.

Mont de Virginie ('Mort de Virginie'?). Belgium, 1824. Large, well-formed, rich violet.

Monteau. Before 1848. Gallica-China hybrid. Medium, double, compact, blackish purple.

Montebella. Before 1834.

Montezuma 80

Monthyon. Before 1848. Large, double, and globular blooms, grayish-rose, mottled purple.

Montigny 80

Mon Trésor. Before 1838. Medium, double, light clear purple, aging to gray-mauve.

Morin de Damas. Carmine blossoms.

Morocco. Before 1834.

Multiplex. Before 1834.

Mutabilis. Blush white. Not the Centifolia of Redouté. If this name was an abbreviated entry for 'Damascena Mutabilis', then possibly yet another name for 'Belle de Cels'.

Myrsa. Before 1848. Large, double, purple-rose.

Nadiska. Prévost, France, 1819. Medium, full, light, vivid pink.

Nanette 80

Nanine. Vétillard, France. Pink with a paler border.

Napoléon 80

Narbonne. Before 1844. Rosy purple. Profuse bloom.

Narcisse de Salvandy 80

Narcisse Desportes. Before 1834.

Natalie de Pronville. Hardy, France, 1824. Large, semi-double, pink, mottled.

Nationale Tricolore. Before 1846. Compact, light crimson, center shaded purple and edged white. Also see **La Nationale'**.

Naturelle. Before 1834. A crimson Gallica.

Nausicaé. Vibert, France, 1817. Large, very full, globular, rose-pink, shaded. Homeric beauty.

Néala 80

Négresse ('Nigritiana' [#1], 'Roi des Belges' 'Superbe en Brun'). Dupont, France, before 1813. Medium, semi-double, velvety deep purple, shaded brown. In Joséphine's collection at Malmaison.

Negro. Before 1834.

Néhala. Vibert, France, 1845. Small, full, purple, spotted rose.

Nelly. Robert, France, before 1848. Mid-sized, full, cupped, well-formed blossoms. Waxlike pale flesh pink.

Nelson. Vibert, France, 1840. Mid-size, double, violet-purple marbled.

Némorin. Deep crimson.

Ne Plus Ultra [#1]. Descemet, France, before 1848. Large, full, vivid rose-pink. Branching growth.

Ne Plus Ultra [#2] ('Glory of the Gardens Pallagi'). Before 1848. Mid-size, semi-double, globular, deep carmine. Profuse bloom, branching growth.

Neptune. Before 1834. Roman god of the sea.

Nero. See 'Néron'.

Néron 81

Nestor 15, **81**

Neuville. Before 1848. Large, very full, compact, rose-pink, shaded.

New Elm-leafed Rose. See 'Nouvelle à Filles d'Orme'.

New Globe Hip ('New Double Globe Hip'). Before 1848. Gallica-Centifolia hybrid.

News 81

New Village Maid ('Nouvelle Rose Rubanée d'Enghien'). Belgium, 1829. Medium size, very double, and compact flowers of white-striped rose-purple. Upright growth. Resembling 'Gallique Panachée' but more double and compact.

Nicollette. Before 1848. Gallica-Centifolia hybrid. Medium, full, cupped, flesh pink.

Nigritiana [#1]. See 'Négresse'.

Nigritiana [#2]. See 'Mme. Christophe'.

Nigritienne. See 'Mme. Christophe'.

Nigrorum. Calvert, France, before 1838. Small, full, very dark velvety purple-violet.

Ninon à Fleurs et Feuilles Panachées. Prévost, France. Dark pink with a paler border.

Ninon de l'Enclos. See 'Joséphine' [#1].

Niobe. See 'Nouveau Triomphe'. Queen of classical story; symbol of grief. Mother of Chloris.

Nisieda. Noisette, France, 1827. Crimson, shaded.

Noble Cramoisie. Robert, France, before 1848. Mid-size, double, crimson.

Noble Fleur. Vibert, France. Pale pink.

Noble Pourpre. Vibert, France, before 1838. Large, very full, light clear crimson-purple.

Noire Couronnée. See 'Gaillarde Marbrée'. A name bestowed on this rose by Joséphine.

Noire de Hollande. Before 1834. Deep crimson.

Noir de Irisée.

Noir Foncée. Before 1834.

Nonpariel. Before 1844. Deep pink.

Non Plus Ultra Pourpre. Before 1834.

Nonsuch. Before 1834.

Normandie ('Rose de Normandie'). Before 1834. Gallica-Phoenicia hybrid.

Nouveau Duc d'York. Sommesson, 1823.

Nouveau Grand Monarque. Before 1838. Medium, full, vivid pink with a paler circumference.

Nouveau Intelligible 82

Nouveau Maheka. See 'Maheca Nova'.

Nouveau Monde 82

Nouveau Rose Marguerite. See 'Comtesse de Baillet'.

Nouveau Rouge. Before 1813. Crimson. In Joséphine's collection at Malmaison.

Nouveau Triomphe ('Roi de Rome' [#1], 'Niobe', 'Don de l'Amitié', 'Eugénie', 'L Aimable Beauté', 'Daphne' [#2]). Prévost, France, 1818. Medium, double, convex, pale, clear pink.

Nouveau Vulcain 82

Nouvelle à Filles d'Orme ('New Elm-leafed Rose'). Vibert, France, 1838. Large, convex, pale pink. Foliage deeply toothed, curled, and undulated.

Nouvelle Bourbon. See 'Nouvelle Provins'.

Nouvelle de Provence. See 'La Triomphante' [#2].

Nouvelle Duchesse d'Orléans. White, shaded violet.

Nouvelle du Jour. Wine crimson.

Nouvelle Favorite. Before 1834.

Nouvelle Gagnée. Before 1813. In Joséphine's collection at Malmaison.

Nouvelle Héloise. See 'Agathe Nouvelle'.

Nouvelle Maheca. See 'Passe Velours'.

Nouvelle Pivoine 82

Nouvelle Provins ('Nouvelle Bourbon'). Before 1848. Medium, double, compact, vivid crimson, shaded purple and edged crimson-purple. Branching growth.

Nouvelle Redouté. Before 1834. Pink blossoms.

Nouvelle Reine Marguerite. See 'Tricolore d'Orléans'.

Nouvelle Rose Marguerite. Flesh pink.

Nouvelle Rose Pavot. Miellez, France, before 1838. Gallica-Centifolia hybrid. Large, crimson center with a pink circumference.

Nouvelle Rose Rubanée d'Enghien. See 'New Village Maid'.

Nouvelle Transparente 82

Novalinska. Before 1848. Gallica-Centifolia hybrid. Mid-size, double, delicate rose pink.

Ober Kempft. Before 1848. Large, doubled, expanded bright rose. Circumference shaded violet. Upright growth.

Octavie [#1] 82

Octavie [#2]. Descemet, France. Historical descriptions of this rose and the one above differ only by hybridizer attribution. Quite possibly, they are the same. If so, 'Octavie' was a survivor of the largest rose rescue in

141

Pourpre Charmant Strié. Hardy, France. Purple, striped white.

Pourpre Couronne. Hardy, France, 1824. Medium, double, violet-purple with a button eye.

Pourpre Cramoisi. See 'Aldegonde' [#2].

Pourpre de Corinthe. Before 1838. Medium, loosely double, bright deep crimson-purple.

Pourpre de Feu. Before 1834.

Pourpre de la Reine. Coquerel, France, before 1838. Large, full, velvety purple with a crimson center. Vigorous.

Pourpre de Paris. Before 1834.

Pourpre de Tyr. See 'Gros Chalons'.

Pourpre de (des?) Vallées. Before 1834.

Pourpre de Vienne. Before 1846. Rose-purple.

Pourpre Foncé. Descemet, France. Deep purple.

Pourpre Marbré . See 'Arlequin'.

Pourpre Mignon. Before 1834.

Pourpre Obscur. See 'Britannicus'.

Pourpre Ponceau. Deep purple.

Pourpre sans Aiguillons. See 'Grandes Divinites'.

Pourpre sans Épines. See 'Grandes Divinites'.

Pourpre sans Pareille. Before 1834.

Pourpre Strié de Blanc. Before 1846. Small, double, reflexed, purple, striped crimson and white. Small, branching growth.

Pourpre Superbe. Before 1834.

Pourpre Triomphant ('Pourpre Triomphale'). van Eeden, Holland, before 1834. Medium, full, vivid crimson-purple.

Pourpre Violet. Before 1834.

Pourpre Violet Marbré. Blackish purple.

Pourpre Violette. Before 1834.

Précieuse [#1]. See 'La Précieuse'.

Précieuse [#2]. Miellez, France. Deep crimson.

Premièr Couronne. Before 1834.

Première Rose. Before 1834.

Président de Sèze   91

Président Dutailley   91

Presque Bleu. Descemet, France. Blackish crimson.

Prince Albert. Bromley, before 1848. Gallica-China hybrid. Mid-size, double, compact blush-pink.

Prince Antoine d'Aremberg. Parmentier, Belgium. Purple.

Prince Charles. Wine crimson.

Prince d'Aremberg. See 'Duc d'Aremberg'.

Prince de Carignan. Miellez, France. Deep crimson blooms.

Prince de Chimay. Parmentier, Belgium, before 1844. Very double, flesh pink blooms with large blush spots.

Prince de la Moskowa. Crimson.

Prince de Ligne. Before 1834. Deep pink, marbled.

Prince de Nassau. Miellez, France. Dark pink.

Prince d'Esterhacy. Before 1834.

Prince Engelbert. Parmentier, Belgium. Lilac pink.

Prince Frédéric   92

Princely. Before 1834.

Prince Régent. Before 1834. Large, very full, cupped, vivid rose. Upright growth.

Princess Amélia ('Princesse Amélie'). Before 1838. Gallica-Centifolia hybrid. Large, loosely double, pink.

Princess Augusta. Before 1848. Gallica-China hybrid. Large, full, cupped, vivid crimson, marbled with purple.

Princess Charlotte. Laffay, France, before 1838. Very double, bright pink with a pale circumference. Perhaps a Gallica-China hybrid.

Princesse ('Rose Princesse'). Hardy, France, 1824. Gallica-Centifolia hybrid. Large, very full, pale pink.

Princesse Alice. Blush white.

Princesse Clémentine. Vibert, France, 1842. Gallica-Centifolia hybrid. Medium, double, compact white. Vigorous growth.

Princesse de Galles. Deep pink.

Princesse de Liévin. Parmentier, Belgium. Deep pink.

Princesse de Nassau   92

Princesse de Portugal ('Princess of Portugal'). Pelletier, France, before 1838. Very large, double, bright cherry-crimson.

Princesse de Salm ('Princess of Salms'). Vibert, France, 1822. Medium, double, pale to light vivid pink.

Princesse de Siam. Violet crimson.

Princesse Eléonore. See 'Belle Eléonore'.

Princesse Marianne. Dark pink flowers.

Princesse Nobilis.

Princess of Portugal. See 'Princesse de Portugal'.

Princess of Salms. See 'Princesse de Salm'.

Princess Scotch. Before 1834.

Princess Victoria. Before 1846. Mid-size, loosely double, expanded, crimson, base of petals purple. Upright growth.

Prince William. Before 1834.

Prinz Frédéric von Preussen. Germany. Lilac.

Professor. Before 1834.

Prolifère. See 'Isabella' [#1].

Promothée. Before 1848. Gallica-China hybrid. Large, full, lilac-rose. From Greek mythology, fire-giver who was chained to Mount Caucasus by Zeus.

Properce. Vibert, France. Purple and violet.

Proserpine. Prévost, France, before 1834. (Perhaps originally from van Eeden.) Medium, full, velvety blackish purple with bronze highlights. Daughter of Demeter/Ceres; wife of Pluto.

Proserpine Nouvelle. Racine, France, before 1838. Medium, very full, very dark purple with a lighter, brighter center.

Protocole. Velvety purple blooms.

Provence à Fleur Comprimée. See 'A Fleurs Comprimées'.

Provins Ancien   92

Provins Flame-colored Rose. Before 1838. Very large, semi-double, vivid crimson, paling to bright cherry-crimson. Reverse of petals paler. Perhaps the same as 'Feu Brillant' [#2].

Provins Marbré   92

Provins Monstreaux. Before 1834. Possibly same as 'Monstrosa'.

Provins Pompon. See 'Pompon' [#1].

Provins Rampant. Before 1834.

Provins Renoncule   92

Provins Rose, Crimson Colored. Before 1838. Medium, double, crimson becoming purple. Probably the same as one of the above listed 'Cramoisi' roses.

Provins Rose with Convex Flowers. Before 1838. Large, very full, pink with large petals.

Provins Rose with Variegated Flowers & Leaves. See 'A Fleurs et Feuilles Marbrée'.

Provins Striée. Before 1834. A striped Gallica.

Prudence. Miellez, France.

Psyche. Vibert, France, 1818. Medium, pale flesh pink.

Vigorous, upright growth. Allegorical personification of the soul; loved by Cupid.

Pucelle de Bergham. Flesh pink.

Pucelle de Bruxelles. See 'La Reine des Roses'.

Pucelle de Cologne. Germany.

Pucelle de Jacques. Jacques, France. Deep purple.

Pucelle de l'Est. Pale pink.

Pucelle de Lille 92

Pucelle d'Enghien.

Pucelle Sadeur. Crimson, shaded.

Pulchra Marmorea [#1]. Before 1846. Vivid rose-crimson, marbled white.

Pulchra Marmorea [#2]. Before 1848. Medium, very full, cupped, rich purple, marbled crimson. Upright growth.

Pulmonaire. Noisette, France. Purple, spotted.

Purple Province Marbled Rose. Prévost, France, 1826. As described by Gore: Mid-size, very double, and quartered blossoms of rich dark purple, streaked with lilac-crimson and violet-gray. This rose would obviously have had a French name; however, it doesn't match any of the above roses with *Pourpre* or *Marbré* in their names.

Purple-Variegated Provins Rose. See 'Ombrée Parfaite'.

Pymaea. Clear, bright crimson.

Pyramidalis Atropurpurea. Before 1834.

Pyramide Agréable. Miellez, France, before 1834. White with a flesh pink center.

Pyramide Pourpre. Before 1834.

Pyramus ('Pyramie'). Racine, France, before 1838. Medium, full, purple. From Ovid's *Metamorphoses*, one of the ill-fated Babylonian lovers.

Pyrrhus. Clear lilac blossoms. Greek warrior at Troy; husband of Hermione.

Quatre Saisons 92

Quatre Saisons d'Italie 15, 93

Queen Adélaïde. Before 1848. Large, double, compact, rich velvety-purple. Upright growth.

Queen of Nigritia. See 'La Predestinée' [#2].

Queen of Roses. See 'La Reine des Roses'.

Queen of the Netherlands. See 'Reine des Pays-Bas'.

Queen of Violets. Before 1844. Well-formed blooms. Fine violet-purple. Perhaps the same rose as 'Reine des Pourpres'.

Quesné. Forest, 1826. Medium, very double, convex, well-formed rich pink with a paler circumference.

Quirinit. Parmentier, Belgium. Strong pink.

Quitterie. Before 1848. Very large, full, cupped, rose-crimson, shaded with mauve-gray. Pales with age. Upright growth.

Rachel. Parmentier, Belgium. Pink, shaded. 19th-century French actress.

Rameau. Miellez, France. Deep pink. French composer.

Randall 93

Randolph. Before 1848. Very large, double, cupped, well-formed, bright pink blooms tinged with blush. Branching growth.

Raphaël. Verdier, France, before 1834. Pink.

Raucourt. See 'Bandeau de Soliman'.

Ravereau. Crimson.

Reboul. Before 1848. Large, double, compact, rich crimson.

Red Mignon. Before 1834.

Red Rose of Lancaster. See 'Officinalis'.

Refulgent. Before 1834. Velvety purple.

Regia Purpurea. Before 1838. Medium, very full, dark purple with a crimson center.

Regina. See 'Sultana'.

Reginae Dicta ('Rose de Reine'). Godefroy, France, 1817. Medium, double, light rose-purple, often marbled.

Regina Nigrorum. See 'La Prédestinée' [#2].

Regulus. See 'Pourpre Charmant'.

Reine Blanche de Belge. See 'Reine des Belges'.

Reine de Belgique. M. Jacques, France, 1832. Gallica-China hybrid. Large, double, globular, rose-lilac.

Reine de Hongrie. Purple blooms.

Reine de Nigritia. See 'La Prédestinée' [#2].

Reine de Perse 93

Reine de Prusse [#1]. See 'Duc d'Angoulême' [#1].

Reine de Prusse [#2]. See 'Duchesse d'Angoulême' [#1].

Reine des Agathes. Agathe Rose. Lilac-pink.

Reine des Amateurs 93

Reine des Belges ('Reine Blanche de Belge'). Before 1834. Gallica-Centifolia hybrid. Medium, double, compact, white. Small upright growth.

Reine des Cerises. Cerise.

Reine des François. Before 1848. Very large and full, cupped, intense rose-crimson, shaded with mauve-gray. Vigorous, pendulous growth. As described by Paul; did he mean "Français" or mistakenly add an *s* to *de*?

Reine des Nègres. See 'Mme. Christophe'.

Reine des Noires. Parmentier, Belgium. Blackish purple.

Reine des Pays-Bas ('Queen of Netherlands'). Belgium, 1824. Medium, velvety crimson. Profuse bloom.

Reine des Pourpres. Purple.

Reine des Roses. See 'La Reine des Roses'.

Reine de Vibert. Vibert, France. Purple.

Reine Marguerite. See 'Tricolore' [#2].

Renoncule. See 'Provins Renoncule'.

Renoncule Admire-moi. Holland.

Renoncule Cartier. Cartier, France. Blackish purple.

Renoncule Noirâtre. Vibert, France. Purple and violet.

Renoncule Ponctuée 93

Renoncule Rose ('Pink Ranonculus'). Before 1838. Small, full, pale pink.

Renoncule Rouge. Dark pink.

Renoncule Violette. See 'Petite Agathe'.

Reverand. Deep pink.

Revenante. Miellez, France. Pale rose-pink with a lilac circumference.

Rex Nigrorum. See 'La Glorieuse' [#1].

Rex Rubrorum. Before 1834. Deep pink.

Riante. Miellez, France. Crimson.

Riche en Fleurs. See 'Belle de Jour Pâle Riche en Fleurs'.

Richelieu. See 'Duc de Richelieu'.

Richesse. Pink and white blossoms.

Richter. Clear wine crimson. Perhaps named after the German author, Jean Paul Richter (1763-1825).

Riego. Before 1848. Gallica-China hybrid. Large, full, globular, light carmine.

Rien ne me Surpasse. Miellez, France, before 1838. Very large, full, well-formed, expanded, vivid crimson. Upright growth.

Rigoulot's Rose. Rigoulot, before 1838. Very large, double,

Rose Varin. See 'Belle de Cels'.

Rose Visqueuse. See 'Mauve'.

Rose with Yellow-nerved Leaves. See 'A Feuilles à nerves Jaunes'.

Rosier de Francfort. See 'Empress Joséphine'.

Rosier de la Malmaison. See 'Quatre Saisons d'Italie'.

Rosier d'El Golea 97

Rosier des Parfumeurs 97

Rosier van de Eeden. See 'De van Eeden'.

Rosine Dupont. Jacques, France, before 1848. Gallica-China hybrid. Large, full, cupped, flesh pink, shaded violet with a white center.

Rouge Admirable [#1]. See 'Pourpre Charmant'.

Rouge Admirable [#2] 97

Rouge Admirable de Bastien. Crimson.

Rouge Agathe. Before 1834. Agathe rose.

Rouge Agréable. See 'Belle Junon' [#2].

Rouge Ardoise. Calvert, France.

Rouge Brillant. See 'Soleil Brillant'.

Rouge Éblouissante. See 'Assemblage des Beautés'.

Rouge Éclatant. Purple crimson.

Rouge Élegante. Dark crimson.

Rouge Favorite. Deep crimson.

Rouge Formidable. See 'Aldegonde' [#1].

Rouge Frappante. Before 1834.

Rouge Gloriante. Purple, veined.

Rouge Luisante. Before 1834.

Rouge Singuliere. van Eeden, Holland, before 1834.

Rouge Superb Actif. Before 1813. Dark crimson. In Joséphine's collection at Malmaison.

Rouget de l'Isle ('Rouget de Lille'). Vibert, France, 1843. Pink, bordered salmon.

Rouge Vermeille. Deep bright crimson.

Rouppe. Parmentier, Belgium. Deep pink.

Royal Bouquet. Before 1846.

Royal Marbré 97

Royal Purple. Before 1834.

Royal Red. Before 1834.

Royal Virgin. Before 1834.

Ruban Doré . See 'Tricolore' [#1].

Rubens. Germany. Lilac-pink.

Ruth 97

Sablée. Vibert, France, 1836. Dark, velvety.

Sacaliger. Robert and Moreau, France, 1838. Velvety crimson.

St. Hélène. Cartier, France. Dark pink.

St. Nicholas 97

St. Patriks. Before 1834.

Salamon [#1]. Cartier, France, before 1838. Large, full, light pink, spotted white.

Salamon [#2]. See 'Duchess of Cornwall'.

Salluste. Robert, France, 1832. Pink spotted.

Salmacis. Vibert, France, 1841. Gallica-Centifolia hybrid. Medium, full, cupped, peach-pink, speckled blush. Upright growth. Nymph of extreme feminine allures. Transformation myth.

Sampson ('Samson'). Miellez, France, before 1838. Gallica-Centifolia hybrid. Large, full, vivid, pink.

Sanchetti 98

Sancho Panza ('Sancho Panza'). Vibert, France, 1843. Large, double, soft peach-pink aging to mauve-gray. Upright growth. Squire of Don Quixote.

Sanquinea. Calvert, France, before 1838. Medium, full, pink, shaded and spotted deep crimson. As the French word *sanguin* means "of blood," perhaps the same as 'Blood'.

Sans Pariel [#1]. Before 1813. In Joséphine's collection at Malmaison. Pale pink.

Sans Pariel [#2]. Purple and crimson.

Saphyrine. Before 1848. Gallica-China Hybrid. Very large, double, violet, shaded crimson. Perhaps with bluish tones.

Sarah. Calvert, France. Pale pink.

Saturne. Miellez, France, before 1834. Purple flowers. Roman deity dethroned by his son, Zeus.

Saudeur. See 'Roi des Roses'.

Scarlet Fire. See 'Scharlachglut'.

Scarlet Four Seasons. See 'Portland Rose'.

Scarlet Glow. See 'Scharlachglut'.

Scharlachglut 9, 16, **98**

Schiffield. Before 1834. Crimson.

Schismaker ('Schrymake'). Parmentier, Belgium, before 1846. Large, very full, cupped, bright velvety purple-violet. Upright growth, glossy foliage. In 1846, Rivers said, "'Schismaker' would almost lead us to

suppose that that grand desideratum, a blue rose, will yet be obtained by cultivators."

Schöenbrunn ('Schönbrun'). Before 1846. Mid-size, very full, cupped, well-formed, brilliant crimson.

Schrymake. See 'Schismaker'.

Scipio. Before 1848. Cupped, well-formed, rich crimson blossoms. Roman general.

Scris Rose. See 'Couronne de Brabant'.

Séguier [#1]. Vibert, France, 1836.

Séguier [#2] 99

Seigneur d'Hartzelaard. Calvert, France, before 1838. Medium, full, convex, dark purple blossom with crimson center.

Semilasso. Before 1848. Gallica-Centifolia hybrid. Large, cupped, crimson-rose, spotted.

Sémonville à Fleurs Doubles. Hardy, France, 1823. Large, full, well-formed, copper-crimson.

Sénat Romain. See 'Duc de Guiche'.

Seoigné. van Eeden, Holland. Before 1834.

Séphora. Robert, France, 1842. Gallica-Centifolia hybrid. Large, double, flesh pink.

Septimus ('Septime'). Before 1838. Medium, full, light crimson-purple, outer petals striped with white.

Septunie. White blushed with flesh pink.

Séraphine. Before 1838. Gallica-Centifolia hybrid. Large, white with a pale flesh center. Top angel.

Seringa. Very deep crimson.

Serné. See 'Rose Serné'.

Sévigné. Vibert, France, 1819. Medium, full, rich crimson edged paler. French beauty and writer.

Sextus Popinius. 1842. Gallica hybrid? Large, doubled, cupped, rose-pink. Vigorous upright growth.

Shakespeare. Before 1846. Large, rose-crimson with a brighter crimson center. According to Paul, possibly same as 'Kean'.

Shigyoku. Medium, full, compact, well-formed, crimson aging to violet. Modern hybrid from Far East(?).

Shiliste de Kersabiac. Before 1848. Large, full, compact, lilac-crimson.

Sidonie. Before 1848. Cupped, blush-pink.

Signeur d'Arclair. Before 1834.

Silas Varin. Before 1834.

Simon Lebouck ('Simon Lebonk'). Before 1848. Mid-size, double, deep crimson with paler clear circumference.

Simonneau. Parmentier, Belgium. Deep velvety purple.

Simple Carnée. Noisette, France. Flesh pink.

Singleton. See 'La Glorieuse' [#1].

Singulière Agathe. Before 1834. Agathe rose.

Siren. Before 1834.

Sirius. Before 1838. Large, full, vivid crimson. Brightest star in the heavens; Orion's faithful hound.

Sir Walter Scott. Before 1846. Large, full, compact, well-formed, rich purplish rose. Scottish novelist and poet.

Sissinghurst Castle 15, **99**

Sky. Before 1848. Mid-size, double, reflexed, purple, shaded rose. Small upright growth.

Slate-colored Rose. See 'Bizarre Triomphant'.

Smith's Seedling. Before 1848. Gallica-China hybrid. Large, full, expanded, carmine.

Sobieksii. Before 1848. Very large, double, compact, crimson, shaded purple. King of Poland (1624-1696).

Soeur Hospitalière. Miellez, France, before 1838. Medium, very full, bluish violet.

Soleil Brillant 99

Soleil Naissant. Dark crimson.

Soliman. Before 1848. Gallica-Centifolia hybrid. Large, doubled, expanded, well-formed, rose color, marbled purple with a paler circumference. Vigorous upright growth.

Sombrieul. Before 1838. Gallica-Centifolia hybrid. Medium, doubled, expanded rich rose-pink, with a rose-blush circumference and spotted white. Small upright growth.

Sophie Cellier. Pink with a blush border.

Sophie Cottin. See 'Mme. Cottin'.

Sophie d'Helemne. Before 1848. Cream.

Sophie Duval. Before 1848. Very large, doubled, compact, well-formed, rose-pink, shaded lilac and violet. Vigorous upright growth.

Sophie Fouquier. Bright cerise.

Sophocle. Flesh pink, tinged green. Greek dramatist.

Souvenir de Kean. See 'Hippolyte'.

Souvenir de l'Impératrice Joséphine. See 'Empress Joséphine'.

Souvenir de Naverin ('Souvenir de Naverino'). Before 1834. Very large, doubled, expanded, pale pink. Vigorous upright growth.

Souvenir des Français. See 'Napoléon'.

Souvenir D'une Mère. Before 1848. Gallica-China hybrid. Very large, full, vivid rose.

Souverain. Before 1848. Large, doubled, expanded, rose-lilac.

Spectabilis. Violet-crimson flowers.

Splendens 100

Spiral. Before 1834. Velvety purple.

Spotted Ranunculus. See 'Renoncule Ponctuée'.

Spotted Violet. See 'Violette Maculata'.

Stadtholder. Before 1848. Gallica-China hybrid. Large, double, compact, blush-pink with a light rose center.

Stella. Before 1846. Pink, shaded white.

Stéphanie Chevrier. Hardy, France, before 1838. Large, very full, flesh pink.

Stéphanie Fouquier. Crimson.

Sterkmanns 100

Stradella. Vibert, France, 1844. Gallica-Centifolia hybrid. Medium, double, rose-pink. Italian composer.

Stratonice. 1845. Medium, full, rich rose, spotted.

Striped Mignon. Before 1834.

Striped Unique. See 'Unique Panachée'.

Striped Velvet. Before 1834. Crimson, striped.

Subnigra. Velvety brownish purple.

Subrotundifolia crenata. See 'La Glorieuse' [#1].

Sully. V. Verdier, France, 1817. Crimson. French statesman and writer (1560-1641).

Sultana 100

Sultane Double. Before 1813. In Joséphine's collection.

Sultane Favorite. See 'Félicie'.

Sultane Mahmond. Before 1834.

Superb Amaranth. Before 1834.

Superbe [#1]. See 'Tricolore Moyenne' [#4].

Superbe [#2]. See 'Couronne Impériale'.

Superbe Cramoisie. See 'Apollon'.

Superbe en Brun. See 'Négresse'.

Superbe Lilloise. Vibert, France, 1825. Crimson.

Superbe Marbrée ('Superb Marbled'). Before 1846.

Medium, double, well-formed, reflexed, bright rose-crimson, marbled purple. Upright growth.

Superbe Violette. Vibert, France, 1825. Violet.

Superb Tuscan. See 'Tuscany Superb'.

Surlet de Chokier. Crimson, shaded.

Surpasse Singleton. See 'La Glorieuse' [#1].

Surpasse Tout 100, 101

Susanna. Before 1846. Light crimson.

Suzanne. Miellez, France, before 1848. Small, doubled, cupped, well-formed, dark rose-lilac blooms in clusters. Branching growth.

Sylphide. Boyau, France, 1842. White and pink with pale pink border. Any in a class of mortal, but soulless, beings supposed to inhabit the air.

Sylvérie. Vibert, France, before 1838. Large, double, vivid pink.

Sylvie. Miellez, France. White. Mother of Romulus and Remus.

Syrius. Cocquerel, France. Crimson flowers.

Taffin. Miellez, France. Bright crimson.

Talbot. Crimson and violet.

Talma. Prévost, France, before 1838. Very double, dark bluish purple, shaded lilac-crimson, edged paler.

Tamerlane. Before 1848. Large, very full, cupped, carmine. Tartar conqueror.

Tancrède. Miellez, France. Dark crimson. Crusader in Tasso's *Jerusalem Delivered*.

Targélie. Before 1848. Gallica-China hybrid. Medium, double, crimson, shaded purple.

Tatius. Wine crimson. King of Sabines.

Télémaque. Before 1848. Large, double, expanded, light crimson, shaded purple. Son of Ulysses.

Télèsilla ('Télèsille'). Vibert, France, 1820. Small, double, light purple, shaded pale violet.

Temple d'Apollon 100

Temple of Apollo. See 'Temple d'Apollon'.

Tendresse Aimable. Before 1834.

Tendresse d'Apollon. Prévost, France. Lilac-pink.

Ténebreuse. Miellez, France. Purple.

Téolinde. See 'Théodolinde'.

Tête de Mort. Pale crimson.

Thais. Noisette, France, before 1838. Agathe rose.

Medium, very double, globular, bright crimson shaded with white. Greek courtesan; mistress of Alexander.

Thalia. Before 1848. Cupped, rich deep pink. One of the three Graces; muse of comedy and bucolic poetry.

Thalie la Gentile   **102**, 103

Théagène. See 'La Pucelle'.

The Bishop   16, **102**, 103

The Lee Rose. See 'Lee' [#2].

Thélèsille. Vibert, France, 1845. Medium, full, crimson-purple, shaded.

Théodolinde ('Téolinde'). Vibert, France, before 1848. Large, double, cupped, bright rose.

Théodore. 1819. Gallica-Centifolia hybrid. Medium, double, rose-pink.

Théodore de Corse. See 'King of Rome'.

The Prince. See 'Le Prince'.

Thérèse. Lixau. Violet-purple.

The Three Magi. See 'Gentil'.

The Wax Rose. See 'Duchesse d'Angoulême' [#1].

The Widow Rose. See 'La Veuve' [#1].

Thornless Violet. See 'Violet sans Aiguillons'.

Thouin. See 'André Thouin'.

Tibulle. Before 1846. Large, double, lilac-crimson, spotted mauve. Vigorous upright growth. Named after the Roman poet, Tibullus.

Tidbit Rose. See 'Conditorum'.

Tigris. Before 1834.

Timarette. Vibert, France, before 1838. Medium, very full, purple-rose, spotted and mottled.

Titan. Before 1834.

Tombeau de Napoléon. Before 1846. Deep crimson with pale circumference.

Tom Jones. Before 1848. Very large, double, vivid rose. Hero of Fielding novel.

Toque Royale. See 'Turban Royal'.

Tour Malakoff. Robert. Lilac-rose. Not to be confused with Soupert's purple Centifolia, 1857. Perhaps the 'Tour Malakoff' ('Tour de Malakoff') in circulation today— so Gallica in coloring and appearance, though tall—is actually Robert's Gallica, and not the Centifolia. Indeed the hues of the rose in cultivation seem closer

to the description of Robert's rose, which might have been a Gallica x Centifolia hybrid.

Toussaint. Deep crimson. Possibly named after the Haitian general and liberator.

Tout Aimable. See 'Enfant de France Nouveau'.

Toutain. Vibert, France, before 1838. Medium, semi-double, mauve-lilac, spotted lilac-crimson. Blossoms in clusters.

Trafalgar. Before 1834.

Transon-Gombault. Before 1848. Large, double, clear crimson with a pale circumference.

Transparante. Miellez, France, before 1834. Pale pink.

Transparante Nouvelle. Before 1834.

Trémière de la Chine. See 'A Fleurs de Rose Trémière de la Chine'.

Trésarin. Calvert, France, before 1838. Medium, double, purple-crimson with a violet circumference.

Trésorier. Before 1848. Mid-size, very full, expanded, crimson, streaked vivid deep purple. Upright growth.

Tricolor de Vazemmes ('Tricolor de Wazemmes', 'Tricolore Superbe'). Before 1846. Small, full, expanded, violet-purple striped with white.

Tricolor de Wazemmes. See 'Tricolor de Vazemmes'.

Tricolore [#1]   103

Tricolore [#2] ('Reine Marguerite'). Vibert, France. Cerise and purple, paling to lilac.

Tricolore de Flandre   103, **104**

Tricolore d'Enghien. Parmentier. Belgium. Carmine and purple striped.

Tricolore d'Orléans ('Nouvelle Reine Marquerite'). Crimson-purple and striped white. Expanded.

Tricolore Moyenne [#1]. Vibert, France, 1841. Pink with a white border and white stripes. Mid-size.

Tricolore Moyenne [#2]. Vibert, France. Stripes of deep pink, white, and purple.

Tricolore Moyenne [#3]. Vibert, France. Mid-size, double, brownish violet, marbled crimson.

Tricolore Moyenne [#4] ('Superbe' [#1]). Vibert, France, 1844. Mid-size, double, violet-purple, spotted white and pink.

Tricolore Moyenne [#5]. Robert, France, 1832. Violet-purple, bordered white and lightly spotted.

Tricolore Pompone. Before 1846. Small, semi-double, expanded, rose-crimson, edged cream and aging to crimson-purple. Small upright growth. Believed to have been a sport of 'Tricolore' [#1].

Tricolore Superbe. See 'Tricolor de Vazemmes'.

Triomphante. Before 1834.

Triomphe d'Angers. Before 1834. Gallica-China hybrid. Large, very full, cupped, vivid carmine, striped white.

Triomphe de Beauté. Before 1846. Mid-size, very full, expanded, well-formed, violet-purple, striped and shaded crimson. Profuse bloom.

Triomphe de Brabant [#1]. Bright crimson.

Triomphe de Brabant [#2]. Mid-sized, doubled, compact, peach-pink blossoms. Vigorous branching growth.

Triomphe de Dusseldorf. Germany. Lilac-pink.

Triomphe de Flore   103

Triomphe de Guerin. Guerin, France, before 1848. Gallica-China hybrid. Large, full, globular, rose-pink with a blush circumference.

Triomphe de Jaussens. Before 1846. Medium, double, cupped, well-formed, bright rose-crimson blossoms shaded purple. Branching growth.

Triomphe de Laqueue. Noisette, France, before 1848. Gallica-China hybrid. Large, doubled, cupped, lilac-rose, veined mauve-gray, with a bright crimson center.

Triomphe de Louvin. Violet-crimson.

Triomphe de Parmentier. Parmentier, Belgium, before 1848. Large, double, violet, shaded edges.

Triomphe de Rennes. Before 1846. Very large, double, expanded, bright crimson, marbled mauve-gray. Upright growth.

Triomphe des Dames. Hardy, France, before 1838. Small, very double, convex, velvety purple, shaded violet.

Triomphe de Sterkmanns. Deep pink.

Triomphe d'Europe. Before 1838. Medium, very full, deep violet-purple, lighter streaks.

Triomphe de Vibert. Vibert, France. Crimson.

Triomphe de Zehler. Before 1848. Medium, full, mauve-gray.

Triomphe Royal. Before 1834. Deep pink.

Triumph of Flora. See 'Triomphe de Flore'.

Tullie. Before 1846. Very large, full, vivid deep rose, spotted and marbled. From legend, Tullie was the wife of Tarquin, the last king of Rome.

Turban Royal ('Toque Royale'). Before 1834. Glowing crimson.

Ulysse. See 'Bandeau de Soliman'.

Unguiculata caryophyllata. Dupont, France, before 1834. Pink.

Uniflore. See 'La Glacée'.

Uniflore Marbrée. Moreau and Robert, France, before 1846. Medium, full, expanded, well-formed, bright rose, spotted white. Upright growth.

Unique Admirable ('Unique Spectabilis'). Descemet, France, before 1834. Gallica-Centifolia hybrid. Medium, double, bright violet-crimson. Possibly the same as 'Beauté Parfaite', which was imported from Holland.

Unique Blanche. Before 1834.

Unique de Bruxelles. 1826. Medium, very full, well-formed, pale pink blooms edged with crimson.

Unique de Hollande. Prévost, France, before 1838. Medium, very full, convex, light clear purple.

Unique Panachée ('Striped Unique'). Before 1834. White, tinged with salmon.

Unique Rouge. Before 1834.

Unique Spectabilis. See 'Unique Admirable'.

Valentine. Vibert, France. Dark pink.

Valentine de Marcellus. Noisette, France, 1827. Violet-crimson blossoms.

Valérie. Pink.

Validatum. See 'Gloire des Pourpres'.

Vallière. See 'La Vallière'.

Valmore Desbordes. Before 1834. Gallica-Centifolia hybrid. Large, double, pale flesh pink.

Van Dael. Before 1838. Large, full, deep, lilac-pink, edged paler.

Vandael (Van Dael's). Before 1848. Gallica-China hybrid. Large, doubled, cupped, purple-crimson, marbled mauve-gray. Not the same as the above or the Tea and Moss roses that bear this name.

Vandyke ('Vandyck', 'Van Dyck'). Parmentier, Belgium, before 1848. Very large, cupped, deep pink.

Van Huyssum. Parmentier, Belgium. Deep crimson.

Variété de Carmin Brillanté. Carmine.

Varin. See 'Belle de Cels'.

Vauban [#1]. Miellez, France, before 1838. Gallica-Centifolia hybrid. Medium, very full, flesh pink. French marshall and military engineer (1633-1707).

Vauban [#2]. Before 1848. Gallica-China hybrid. Large, full, cupped, crimson-purple.

Velours Cramoisie. Before 1834.

Velours d'Enghien. Violet blossoms.

Velours Episcopal. Before 1848. Gallica-China hybrid. Medium, double, globular, vivid crimson, shaded violet-purple.

Velours Noir. Dupont, France. Violet.

Velours Pourpre Nouveau. Prévost, France, 1828. Deep velvety purple.

Velours Violet. Vibert, France, 1825. Gallica-China hybrid. Dark violet.

Velutina. van Eeden, Holland, 1810. Semi-double, velvety violet-purple blossom with center of gold stamens.

Velutiniflora. See 'Velutinaeflora'.

Velvet-Violet Ranunculus. See 'Britannicus'.

Venetian. Before 1834.

Vénus. Vibert, France, 1845. Gallica-Centifolia hybrid. Large, double, white, shaded lilac.

Vénus de Medicis. Before 1848. Rose-pink with a blush rose circumference.

Vénus Mère. See 'Bouquet Charmant'.

Venustus. Calvert, France, before 1838. Medium, full, dark rich crimson-purple shaded blackish.

Vermillon. Before 1834.

Vernon. Crimson-purple.

Verte Blanche. Hardy, France, before 1838. Large, very full, pale pink tinged with greenish-white.

Vesta. See 'Feu de Vesta'.

Veturie. Vibert, France, before 1838. Large, very full, rich rose-crimson.

Vicomte de Spoelberg. Deep crimson.

Victoire Bizarre. Before 1846. Bluish violet-crimson, mottled white.

Victoire de Bragance. See 'Dorothée' [#1].

Victoire de Tracy. Laffay, France, before 1848. Gallica-China hybrid. Large, full, dark purple, shaded crimson.

Victoire de Waterloo ('Waterloo'). Before 1848. Large, semi-double, cupped, deep lilac.

Victorine. Before 1834. Bluish tones.

Victorine la Couronne. Before 1813. In Joséphine's collection at Malmaison.

Victory. Before 1834.

Victory of Braganza. See 'Dorothée' [#1].

Vidua. Before 1848. Vivid crimson.

Villagoise Parée. Before 1848. Very full, pale crimson.

Vinck Noir. Blackish purple blossoms.

Vingt-neuf Julliet. See 'Coccinea Superba'.

Vingt-Sept Mai. Dark crimson.

Violacea. See 'La Belle Sultane'.

Violacea Maxima. Before 1834.

Violet. Before 1834. An Agathe rose.

Violet à Grandes Fleurs. Violet with a white border.

Violet Bronze. Glowing purple.

Violet Crémer ('Violet de Crème'). 1824. Large, very full, expanded, rich rose-crimson, shaded dark violet-purple. Upright growth.

Violet de Belgique. Before 1848. Gallica-China hybrid. Large, double, violet.

Violet de Canterbury. Violet-pink.

Violet de Crème. See 'Violet Cremer'.

Violet de Douai. Deep crimson.

Violet Incomparable. Violet.

Violet Magnifique. Violet.

Violet Merveilleux. Miellez, France. Dark violet.

Violet Picotée. See 'Picotée'.

Violet sans Aiguillons ('Thornless Violet'). Before 1848.

Gallica-China hybrid. Medium, full, expanded, dark purple with a bright crimson center.

Violette Agréable. Descemet, France, before 1834. Violet.

Violette Brillanté. See 'Aldegonde' [#1].

Violette Curieuse. Before 1834.

Violette et Rouge. Before 1834. Mauve.

Violette Maculata ('Spotted Violet'). Before 1834. Medium, semi-double, deep rich violet, spotted and paling with age.

Violette Nouvelle. Before 1834.

Violette Pontuée. Vibert, France. Violet, spotted.

Violette Rouge. Violet, crimson, and white.

Violette Royale. Before 1834.

Violette sans Pareille. Before 1834.

Violette Superb. Before 1834.

Violettte Supérieur. Before 1834.

Violet Virginie. Vibert, France, 1825. Violet.

Virginale. Before 1834.

Virginie. Before 1848. Large, double, cupped, rose-pink.

Virginie Zechler. Before 1848. Gallica-China hybrid. Large, double, cupped, bright rose, tinged lilac.

Visqueuse. See 'Mauve'.

Vitex Spinosa. See 'Belgica Rubra'.

Vitruvius. Before 1848. Medium, full, cupped, even clear pink. Branching growth. Roman authority on architecture.

Volème. Girardon, France. Mauve-crimson.

Volney. Laffay, France, before 1848. Gallica-China hybrid. Large, full, lilac-rose.

Vulcain. Before 1834. Gallica-China hybrid. Mid-size, full, vivid crimson shaded maroon. Roman deity of fire and metals.

Wargny. Pink flowers.

Wariricus. See 'Pharericus'.

Washington. Before 1848. Medium, full, cupped, crimson, marbled violet-purple.

Waterloo. See 'Victoire de Waterloo'.

Wawerley. Dark crimson.

Wax Rose. See 'Duchesse d'Angoulême' [#1].

Wellington. See 'Lord Wellington'.

Wez. Lilac-pink.

Wilberforce. Circa 1840. Gallica-Centifolia hybrid. Dark crimson-purple. British statesmen and writer.

William Grant   108, **109**

William Tell. See 'Guillaume Tell'.

William the Fourth. Before 1848. Large, full, expanded, bright crimson with a blush-lilac circumference. Pendulous growth.

Wood Pigeon. England. Before 1838.

Xénophon. Vibert, France, 1816. Purple. Athenian historian and general.

Yolande Fontaine. Before 1848. Gallica-China hybrid. Mid-size, double, globular, dark black-violet.

York Élégant. Flesh pink blossoms.

Ypsilante. See 'Ipsilanté'.

Zaire. Vibert, France, 1817. Large, semi-double, rose-purple aging bluish.

Zenaide Delezenne. Before 1848. Large, cupped, vivid rose-pink.

Zénaire. Dubourg, France. Purple, spotted white.

Zenobia. Vibert, France, 1837. Pink. Grown at Roseraie de l'Haÿ before 1900. Queen of Palmyra, ancient city in Syria.

Zetella. Before 1848. Gallica-China hybrid. Medium, double, globular, clear rose.

Zoë   108

Zumalacáréguy. Before 1848. Mid-size, double, expanded, even rose-pink, blush-lilac with age, and occasionally striped white. Branching growth.

Suzanne Verrier currently owns and operates a saltwater farm and nursery in Maine, specialising in unusual and rare roses. She is also a consulting rosarian, lecturer on roses, and garden designer. Her articles and photographs on roses and other garden topics have appeared in numerous publications. Photographs of her personal and nursery display gardens have been featured in various books and magazines.

Readers wishing to contact the author should address their correspondence to her at North Creek Farm, 24 Sebasco Road, Phippsburg, Maine, USA 04562.

Also by the author: *Rosa Rugosa*, available from Firefly Books.

> "The chief danger of this book is that the gardener will be tempted
> to grow every rose in it . . ."   —Henry Mitchell